KEYS TO
INVESTING IN
YOUR 401(K)

KEYS TO INVESTING IN YOUR 401(K)

Warren Boroson
Instructor
Rutgers University, The New School,
Bergen Community College

BARRON'S

All inquiries should be addressed to:
Barron's Educational Series, Inc.
250 Wireless Boulevard
Hauppauge, New York 11788

Library of Congress Catalog Card Number 94–10410

International Standard Book No. 0–8120–1873–7

Library of Congress Cataloging-in-Publication Data

Boroson, Warren.
  Keys to investing in your 401(k) / Warren Boroson.
        p. cm.—(Barron's business keys)
  Includes index.
  ISBN 0-8120-1873-7
  1. 401(k) plans. I. Title II.Series
HF5549.5.C67B67 1994
332.024'01—dc20   94-10410
                                                            CIP

PRINTED IN THE UNITED STATES OF AMERICA
4567   9770   987654321

CONTENTS

1

MISTAKES WITH
401(K) PLANS

A 401(k) plan is so vital to your being able to retire comfortably, so essential to your financial health in general, that the most important thing for people who can invest in such plans to know, first off, is what mistakes they should avoid making.

The worst mistake is to invest in volatile securities (like stocks), then to sell in a panic if their prices decline.

To put it another way, the worst mistake is for a novice to make an investment suitable for sophisticated investors. Stocks may be wonderful investments—for sophisticated people. Guaranteed investment contracts (Key 30) may be inappropriate investments for sophisticated people—but not for novices.

No other mistake is so costly as buying volatile securities if you aren't prepared to cope with volatility—whether the other mistake is investing too conservatively, not investing enough, whatever. No other mistake is so expensive.

Another common and expensive mistake that people make is not taking advantage of a 401(k) plan when they have one available. Right now, only 60 to 65 percent of those Americans eligible for 401(k)s have chosen to participate. More than one-third of the people eligible are missing out on one of the truly golden opportunities of their lives.

Unfortunately, the well-to-do are more likely to participate than the less well-to-do, who would probably benefit more. By and large, the higher-paid an employee covered by a 401(k) plan is, the more likely that person is to salt money away into a plan. Someone earning over $50,000 a year is roughly twice as likely to participate than someone earning less than $15,000.

Who Participates?

Salary	401(k) Participation
Over $50,000	81%
$30,000–$49,999	67%
$25,000–$29,999	59%
$20,000–$24,999	57%
$15,000–$19,999	50%
$10,000–$14,999	42%
$5,000–$9,999	33%
Less than $5,000	22%

Source: *Financial Planning*, August 1991

Third serious mistake: not taking advantage of employers' contributions.

Many employers match their workers' contributions, up to a certain amount. That is, if you contribute 3 percent of your salary to your 401(k) plan, your employer may match your contribution by adding an extra 1.5 percent to your 401(k) plan. That's a 50 percent return on some of your money. It's not just a free lunch. It's a free banquet. It's money in the bank, manna from heaven.

Yet many people don't even put the minimum amount of money into their 401(k) plans that would be matched by their employers!

Even people with both money and brains may foolishly ignore 401(k) plans. B. Douglas Bernheim, a Princeton economist, reports that Stanford University once began offering an "extraordinarily generous" plan under which the university contributed $2 for every dollar an employee put into the plan, up to 15 percent of the employee's earnings. "That's free money," he noted, "and nobody should turn that down. But an astonishing number of Stanford faculty—and these are well-informed, educated people—chose not to participate."

Of course, you may believe that you can't spare any of your salary, not even $100 or $500 a year—even though $500 a year is less than $10 a week. Still, as the saying goes, if you can't live on what you have, you cannot live on 5 percent less, either. So invest 5 percent.

There's no other investment you will ever encounter that may bless you so painlessly with a 50 percent or 100 percent return on part of your money. So beg or borrow (draw the line at stealing), but put at least enough money into your 401(k) plan so that your employer matches every cent you salt away.

Fourth bad mistake: not salting away more money. A survey sponsored by Merrill Lynch & Co. found that only about one third of the participants contributed the maximum that they can (the maximum that's tax-deferred changes every year, in line with inflation). The *least* that you should contribute is the amount that's matched by your employer's own contribution.

Fifth mistake: not putting enough money into the stock market.

Yes, the stock market is scary. It's volatile; it can bounce up and down like a yo-yo. It can sink down and remain down for what seems like eternity. (See Key 19.) Yet, over the years, the stock market has rewarded investors more generously than fixed-income investments, cash equivalents (like money market funds), precious metals, antiques and collectibles, and so forth.

"To be investing almost exclusively in the safest asset available [guaranteed investment contracts]," Bernheim observes, "means that these people will get much lower returns than if their pension portfolio were professionally managed"—that is, if someone who knew what he or she was doing were managing the money.

Sixth mistake: putting too much money into your employer's stock.

Actually, the real mistake here is not being diversified enough—not having enough money in a basket of stocks.

Your employer may be a wonderful employer, fair and generous. The company may be a thriving enterprise, making money hand over fist. The stock may even be selling for less than it should.

It's still a bad idea to have one stock dominating your portfolio—even if you can buy the stock cheaply.

The stocks of great companies can take great falls. IBM went from $178 a share a few years ago to $40 a share recently.

How many stocks must you own to be fairly well diversified? The answer, according to a 1990 study, is twenty. With twenty stocks, if one stock falls off the table, you're not going to suffer the pains of hell. But even with twenty, there's a 10 percent chance that your portfolio will underperform the stock market (as represented by the Standard & Poor's 500 Stock Index) by 10 percent.

That study didn't consider that the twenty stocks might be in different industries, in which case you might not need so many as twenty. So let's say that you should own fifteen stocks in a variety of industries. What amount should any one stock compose of your portfolio? About 7 percent tops. So, by the same logic, your employer's stock shouldn't make up more than 7 percent of your investments. If it does, start cutting back.

Seventh mistake: not having a guide to how your money should be invested—an "asset allocation model."

How much should you have in stocks, in bonds, and in cash? The answer depends upon your age, your goals, your overall prosperity, your "risk tolerance." You should sit down and decide how your money should be divided, then roughly follow that model. (See Keys 33–38.)

Eighth mistake: investing too aggressively.

If you're approaching retirement, obviously you shouldn't be 80 percent in the stock market—unless you don't need your 401(k) money to live on and you intend to leave it all to your children, your grandchildren, or someone else decidedly younger.

Who would choose to invest too aggressively? Perhaps people who don't know that between 1972 and 1974 the stock market, as represented by the Dow Jones Industrial Average, lost 48 percent of its value. And that if you had invested in a well-diversified basket of stocks in 1929, before the great crash, you wouldn't have received your money back for eight years.

Only the very bravest people, it has been said, should have as much as 80 percent of their investments in the stock market.

Ninth mistake: Blindly following the leaders.

Let's say that stocks did fabulously in the past three

months, fixed-income investments did woefully. So you shift your asset allocation, moving toward stocks and away from bonds. The next three months, stocks go to heck in a hand-basket and bonds soar to the skies. So you change your positions again . . . .

This is known as "market-timing," trying to avoid bear markets (when prices go down) and enjoy bull markets (when prices go up).

Market-timing has a foul reputation. One clever investor has said that if anyone could ever correctly divine whether stocks will be going up or down, he or she would own the world in three months—"One month with leverage." (*Leverage* means borrowing money to invest.)

Actually, market-timing can be successful. But practitioners who don't lose their shirts tend to make fairly modest shifts between stocks, bonds, and cash, not frequent and drastic changes. So, if you have an opportunity to invest in a market-timing fund with a good track record, consider it.

But don't market-time on your own. Most people should consider themselves long-term investors, ready to accept bear markets along with bull markets.

Tenth mistake: not rebalancing.

Let's say that you think you should be 60 percent in stocks, 40 percent in fixed-income investments. A few years elapse. The stock market does wonderfully, the bond market does frightfully. You're now 80 percent in stocks, 20 percent in bonds. You're probably too much exposed to the risk of the stock market at this point. Cut back on your stocks—and either add to your bonds or put money into cash equivalents, like money market funds. (See Key 38.)

Eleventh mistake: Withdrawing money from your 401(k) plan when you don't have to. (See Keys 41–44.)

Of those people who received lump-sum distributions in 1992 from their pension plan because of retirement or a job change, one third spent all of it; the rest saved some and spent some; only 11 percent rolled the entire balance over into another retirement plan.

There are other dreadful mistakes investors can make, but these may be the eleven worst.

2

THE CASE FOR 401(K) PLANS

A 401(k) plan can shower you with blessings.

First off, the money you put in is tax-deferred (up to a yearly limit, $9,240 in 1994).

Your earnings are also not taxed—until you withdraw the money.

Your employer may even toss some money into your pot—perhaps 25 cents for every dollar you contribute, up to 7 percent of your salary (which might be $30,000). So, if you contribute $2,100, your employer may kick in $525. That's $2,100 multiplied by .25. And that's a 25 percent return on your money—which hasn't even started working for you!

When you add your employer's matching contributions and any after-tax deposits you make, the yearly limit is $30,000—or less if your plan sets its own limit on what you can contribute.

The highest amount of earnings that can be considered in determining how much you can put into your 401(k) is $150,000.

Generally, you can salt more away into a 401(k) plan than a deductible individual retirement account.

A chief advantage of 401(k) and other retirement-savings vehicles is that you aren't taxed on the money you put away. Here's how much you might save in a tax-deferred investment as opposed to a taxable investment:

The Benefits of Tax-Deferment

	Tax-Deferred	Taxable
Year 1	$2,200	$2,200
Year 5	$13,431	$12,271
Year 10	$35,062	$29,400
Year 15	$69,899	$53,314
Year 20	$126,005	$86,697

Difference: $39,308.

This chart compares the growth of tax-deferred annual investments with similar taxable investments over twenty years. Assumptions: average annual total return of 10 percent, reinvestment of all dividends and capital gains, and a 31 percent tax bracket. Source: Founders Funds.

If you can show good reason, you may even borrow from your 401(k) plan—and even permanently withdraw some of your money before reaching age 59½ (the official age when you're able to withdraw your money without penalty). But your particular plan must authorize these transactions.

If those aren't enough incentives for you to invest in a 401(k) plan, here's another:

When you approach retirement, you may find that you need a lot more retirement money than you had suspected. Today's young people probably won't have it as good as the older generation.

- In the 1980s, the older generation benefited from rapidly rising house prices. Young homeowners certainly won't enjoy the same property appreciation. In fact, many young people who bought houses in the late 1980s have suffered mercilessly, and their residences may not even be worth the amount they still owe on their mortgages.

- "Because many of today's workers defer marriage and parenthood until well into their 30s or later, they may face all at once the expenses [that] families once [were able to] spread over several decades, making it harder to save for retirement," reports Mary H. Cooper in *CQ Researcher* ("Paying for Retirement," Nov. 5, 1993).

- With the population growing older, the pool of young people paying for the Social Security benefits of older people is shrinking. The qualifying age for Social Security recipients has been moved up; it may be moved up again. Social Security benefits of the well-to-do are now subject to taxes; in the future, those taxes may be even more severe.

- People are living longer—and spending more time in retirement.

- Many companies, especially small ones, are replacing their "defined benefit" retirement plans with plans that shift most of the financial burden to the employee, via "defined contribution" plans, like 401(k)s. With a defined contribution plan, the employee must decide whether to invest—and how much—and what to invest in. The dangers here are that (1) employees may choose not to take advantage of their 401(k) plans; and (2) they may invest their money in the plans too conservatively or (less likely) too aggressively.

One estimate is that 401(k) plans will provide about 50 percent of the retirement income for people retiring in the year 2012, compared with about 15 percent for current retirees (Howard Johnson & Co., in *Fortune* magazine, Dec. 28, 1992).

All of which argues for people to be more generous than ever in saving for their retirements, and to start earlier.

Yet the evidence that Americans are doing the right thing isn't there.

People in their 30s and 40s, warns B. Douglas Bernheim, an economics professor at Princeton University, must triple their rate of savings to avoid a sharp decline in their living standards when they retire.

Yet 55 percent of America's 94.8 million workers don't even have pension coverage, the Department of Labor reported in 1990. Even among those who do, the savings rate is low. The amount of disposable income (money available for spending or saving) that Americans set aside for savings has dropped from 7.8 percent in the 1970s to less than 5 percent during the past seven years, according to Marc E. Lackritz, president of the Securities Industry Association.

Sources of Retirement Income
Here is where workers expect their retirement income to come from:

Employer pension/retirement plans:	28%
Social Security:	26%
Personal savings, life insurance, investments, other assets	16%
401(k) plans, thrift plans	14%
IRAs	10%
Tax-sheltered annuities	6%

Based on a survey of 1,000 full-time employed adults by Pulse Surveys of America.

3

WHAT THE TERMS MEAN

Both **401(k) plans and 403(b) plans** enable employees to save for their retirement and enjoy the benefit of having the money they put away go untaxed until they take it out.

They are called "defined contribution plans" because employees can squirrel away a certain (defined) amount of money each year. The amount that they can put into such a plan is the "contribution."

But 403(b) plans are open only to employees of public schools, churches, and certain tax-exempt organizations. These employees are not permitted to participate in 401(k) savings plans. (457 plans are for employees of the federal, state, and local government.)

Other key differences between 403(b) and 401(k) plans:

- Workers who take part in 403(b) plans are currently allowed to make larger annual contributions than people in 401(k) plans;
- Employees in 403(b) plans who accumulated money in their accounts before 1987 can delay receiving their distributions until they reach age 75. Employees in 401(k) plans must begin receiving their money by age 70½.
- People who receive distributions from 401(k) plans may be eligible for a reward when they take their money out: they may be able to take advantage of five-year or ten-year income averaging, which should lower their tax bite. This is not the case with distributions from 403(b) plans.

Equity means ownership. When you encounter the word, usually it means "stocks." An "equity" fund is a mutual fund composed of stocks. (You may also have heard the word in the phrase "home equity loan," a loan that uses your house as collateral. Here, "equity" means your free-and-clear ownership of the house.)

Stocks give you part ownership in a corporation. If you own ten shares of AT&T, for example, you are one of the owners of AT&T. Among other things, you are entitled to receive dividends—if the corporation is actually paying dividends. The prices of stocks typically bob up and down day after day, depending on what people are willing to buy or sell the shares for. If a company is prospering and raises its dividend, for example, the stock's price will probably go up. If the company is being savaged by the competition and it may have to cut or abolish its dividend, the price will probably go down.

If stocks are ownership, fixed-income investments (loosely called **bonds**) are "loanership." You just lend money to a corporation or a bank or an insurance company, and get regular interest. Interest differs from dividends in that dividends are more likely to change—to be raised or cut or abolished. On the other hand, bond prices are less likely to rise or fall as much as stock prices. If you pay $10,000 for a bond, you will receive only your $10,000 back at **maturity**—maybe in five, ten, twenty, or thirty years. Stocks don't mature. But there's no guarantee that you'll receive back whatever money you invested in a stock.

Mutual funds are investment companies that buy stocks or bonds or both. An equity mutual fund gives you a variety of stocks—along with someone (a manager) who decides what to buy, what to sell, what to pay and what to receive, and when.

With a fixed-income mutual fund, you can buy a variety of bonds—Treasury securities from the U.S. Government, bonds from corporations that are thriving (investment-grade bonds), bonds from corporations under a cloud (junk or high yield bonds), mortgage-backed securities, and so forth. You also get a manager who decides what to buy and what to sell, what to pay and what to receive, and when.

Money market funds buy short-term debt obligations. These funds are very safe but they won't normally make you much money. Money market funds keep their price per share fixed at $1, and if interest rates go up, they just lower their yields in order to maintain the share price at $1. (Another term for price per share is **net asset value**.)

Guaranteed investment contracts are like certificates of deposit you buy at banks—but you buy these from insurance companies. Like money market funds, they are very safe but they normally won't make you much money. (See Key 30.) In some plans, you cannot sell your GICs and move into other fixed-income investments, such as money market funds. This is to keep investors from selling GICs when interest rates on money market funds are rising.

Cash equivalents are any investment that can readily be turned into cash—without your losing much, if any, money. Any fixed-income investment that matures in less than a year is considered a cash equivalent. Examples: a one-year CD, money market funds, Treasury bills, one-year guaranteed investment contracts.

Asset allocation means how much you invest in stocks, bonds, and cash. A sort of all-purpose model: 50 percent in stocks, 40 percent in bonds, 10 percent in cash or cash equivalents.

Rebalancing means rejiggering your portfolio if your asset allocation goes out of whack. If you want to be 50 percent in stocks, but the market has soared and you're now 60 percent in stocks, you might cut back your stocks and move more money into fixed-income investments and cash equivalents.

Market-timing means trying to avoid **bear markets** (when investment prices sink) and to enjoy **bull markets** (when prices climb). It is the Holy Grail of investing—desirable, difficult, and dangerous.

Dollar-cost averaging means investing regular amounts of money over regular periods of time. That way, you don't buy when the prices of whatever you're buying are unusually high, ripe for a fall. This applies to both stocks and bonds. If you regularly put money into a retirement plan, you're in effect practicing dollar-cost averaging.

Qualified means that contributions to a retirement plan are tax-deductible, and you don't pay taxes on the money. With an IRA, a $2,000 contribution may be subtracted from your taxable income. With a 401(k) plan, your contribution doesn't appear as income on your W-2 form. But you do pay Social Security taxes on 401(k) contributions, and one state

11

(Pennsylvania) taxes 401(k) contributions. Some cities also tax the contributions.

Risk tolerance means how readily you can cope with volatility—and volatility means the ups and downs of an investment. Your risk tolerance obviously depends, to a large extent, on your investment experience and your sophistication.

A **portfolio** comprises all your investments—stocks, bonds, CDs, limited partnerships, whatever. You can have a tax-sheltered portfolio (IRAs, 401[k]s, Keoghs) and a taxable or private portfolio.

A **Certified Financial Planner** is someone who has passed a test to give financial advice and has several years of experience.

4

VARIETIES OF RETIREMENT PLANS

Retirement plans generally let you to postpone paying taxes on income that you sock away for your old age.

Some employer-sponsored tax-favored savings plans—like 401(k)s—are the new kids on the block. They differ from the older "defined benefit" plans in that most of the contributions are made by the employees themselves; the contributions are voluntary; and the employees must decide for themselves how the money is to be invested.

Employees can put away any amount up to a fixed percentage of their earnings. In other words, your contribution is *defined*, or spelled out. Most employers—86 percent of those with 401(k) plans—match these contributions with smaller amounts, up to a percentage (usually 6 percent) of an employee's salary.

With a defined-contribution plan, you aren't guaranteed the amount you will receive later on. The amount you receive will depend on how you invest your money—wisely or foolishly, aggressively or conservatively. With the older defined-benefit plan, your employer invested your money and promised that you would receive a certain amount. Your benefit (what you would receive) was defined.

Employees in defined-contribution plans typically have at least three choices of where to put their money: stocks, fixed-income investments (like guaranteed insurance contracts), and a combination of stocks and bonds (a "balanced" fund).

If your plan permits, you can borrow money from your defined contribution plan before you reach age fifty-nine and a half. (After that age, there's no penalty.) You won't owe income taxes on the money you borrow provided that you do pay it back.

13

Other varieties of defined contribution plans, besides 401(k)s, are

- 403(b) plans for employees of nonprofit, charitable, religious, or educational organizations.
- Section 457 plans for state and local government employees; and
- federal thrift savings plans for employees of the federal government.

Only 45 percent of American workers in the private sector—employed and unemployed—were covered by retirement plans in 1990, according to the Department of Labor. Of them, about 17 percent were covered only by defined-contribution plans; 13 percent by the older defined-benefit plans; and 15 percent by both defined-contribution and defined-benefit plans.

Defined-benefit plans guarantee monthly benefits to employees. The employers decide how the pension money is to be invested, and they are responsible for investing the money prudently.

People who take part become "vested" (entitled to the benefits they have earned) typically after up to five years of work. The normal retirement age is sixty-five, but employees can retire as early as age fifty-five, depending on the plan, and receive 62 percent of the benefit they have earned. The size of the benefits usually depends on the number of years you have worked, along with your average earnings during the last years you work.

Keogh or **HR-10 plans** are for the self-employed, including freelancers who are covered by retirement plans from their employers. A "profit-sharing" Keogh allows you to defer paying taxes on 13 percent of your self-employment income, up to a $30,000 contribution a year. You must set up a Keogh plan before the end of the year for which you want to salt away retirement money, although you need not put in any money until April 15 of the following year.

Simplified Employee Pensions are similar to other defined-contribution plans, but without all the paperwork. You can set up a SEP in the same year you make a contribution. To participate, you don't necessarily have to be self-employed.

See the next Key for information on Individual Retirement Accounts.

Schematic of How 401(k) Plans Work

Plan	401(k)
Available	Employees of for-profit businesses
Best for	Everyone
Maximum contribution	Up to $9,240 in 1994
Tax breaks on contributions	Yes
Tax breaks on earnings	Yes
Company contributions	Varies, but usually up to 6% of salary
Fees	Usually 1%–1.5% of assets every year
Early withdrawals*	In cases of hardship
Investment options	Usually 3 to 10

*10% tax penalty on withdrawals before age 59.5 unless due to death or disability

5

401(K) PLANS VS. IRAs

The Superiority of 401(k)s. 401(k) plans are typically much better than Individual Retirement Accounts, and given a choice, you should spring for a 401(k) or 403(b) plan. Here are the reasons:

- Whereas the highest tax-deductible amount that you can salt away into an IRA in one year is $2,000 (or $2,250 for a spousal IRA), you may be able to put four times as much into a 401(k) plan—and even more into a 403(b) plan. The theoretical maximum for a 401(k) is around $9,240 now. In 1990, it was $7,979; in 1991, $8,475; in 1992, $8,728; in 1993, $8,994. (But the $9,240 maximum may not be permitted if the plan discriminates in favor of highly paid employees, or if a complex rule, called Section 415, limits contributions.)

- Your employer may contribute to your 401(k) plan; many employers fork over 50 cents for your dollar, up to a limit (such as up to $6,000 of your total contribution).

- You may be able to borrow the money in your 401(k) plan—something that you cannot do with an IRA.

- In certain circumstances, you can withdraw the money from your 401(k) or 403(b) plan before age 59½. This would be the case if you withdraw the 401(k) money to pay certain medical expenses. To qualify, the expenses must be tax-deductible. That means that they must exceed 7.5 percent of your adjusted gross income. (Adjusted gross income is the amount on the last line of page one of Form 1040, the standard federal tax form.) Another case where you can withdraw 401(k) money early: if you're disabled.

- If you withdraw your 401(k) money in a lump sum (all at once) when you retire, you can use a special tax break called "forward averaging." This allows you to pay taxes on that money as if you had withdrawn it over the course of five years, rather than in just one year. That should lower the tax bite, simply because you may wind up in a lower tax bracket.

- One final benefit of a 401(k) plan: some mutual fund families that normally charge a load (sales charge) may drop the charge when people invest via a 401(k) plan.

Tax Aspects. People may think, erroneously, that there are important differences between the deductibility of a 401(k) plan and a deductible IRA.

Not so.

With a 401(k) plan, the money is automatically taken out of your paycheck to go into your retirement plan. The money that's removed isn't taxed (apart from Social Security taxes). The 401(k) money also isn't added to the income on the W-2 Form that you receive in January or February in the succeeding year.

With an IRA, on your tax return you declare the amount of the deduction (on line 24 of Form 1040), so that a corresponding amount of your taxable income escapes taxation.

Tax-wise, the major difference between 401(k)s and IRAs is that 401(k)s are a bit simpler to deal with. There's less paperwork. Things are done automatically.

The Case for IRAs. IRAs have advantages, too. Right now, you probably have a far wider variety of investment choices with IRAs. Certain 401(k) plans give you very limited choices—in some plans, only guaranteed investment contracts.

Also, with IRAs you can move in and out of different investments very readily. If you arrange a trustee-to-trustee transfer (you instruct a brokerage firm or mutual fund, say, to handle the transaction directly), you can make as many changes as you wish—without paying income taxes plus the normal 10 percent IRS tax penalty. If you instruct the current custodian of your IRA to send the money to you, and you move it into a rollover IRA within 60 days, you also won't have to pay taxes and a 10 percent tax penalty. But you're limited to one tax-free rollover a year.

With a 401(k) plan, your ability to switch your investments is usually limited. Many employers, for example, let you make changes only once every three months.

The Labor Department wants employers to make a wider variety of investments available to 401(k) plan investors, and also to allow an investor to shift between investments more frequently.

Only certain people can still deduct from their income all or part of their contributions to an IRA. Employees not cov ered by employer-sponsored retirement plans—or who (if unmarried) earn up to $25,000 a year or who (if married) earn up to $40,000—can deduct up to $2,000 a year that they put into an IRA. Workers with higher earnings can take a percentage of the $2,000 deduction. The cutoff points: up to $35,000 earnings for singles and $50,000 for married couples.

401(k)s Plus IRAs. In certain circumstances, you can have both a deductible IRA and a 401(k) plan. Normally, you cannot have a deductible IRA if you (or your spouse) have access to a company retirement plan, like a 401(k). The exception: if your adjusted gross income is $40,000 or less (for couples) or $25,000 or less (for individuals or heads of households).

Another instance where you can have a 401(k) plan as well as other retirement plans: when you have income from self-employment. With the freelance income, you can set up a HR-10 (Keogh) plan or a Simplified Employee Pension plan.

6

HOW TYPICAL IS YOUR 401(K) PLAN?

A 1991 survey of 171 companies by the Bankers Trust Company, one of the nation's largest full-service providers of defined contribution plans, found:

- of the retirement plans, 88 percent were savings plans with a 401(k) feature;
- the plans offered, on average, four or more funds;
- an "equity index", an "active equity", and a "balanced" fund were increasingly the funds offered.

An equity index is a stock fund, a replica of the stock market as a whole, typically the Standard & Poor's 500 Stock Index.

An active equity fund is also composed of stocks, but it's not just a replica of the S&P 500 Stock Index. It contains stocks of companies that the manager thinks are growing or are undervalued, or both, and will outperform the S&P 500. Typically the manager buys and sells far more often than an index fund would.

A balanced fund holds both stocks and bonds—typically 60 percent stocks, 40 percent bonds. Such a fund is usually more stable than a fund that consists entirely of stocks, and it returns more than a bond fund because of its exposure to stocks.

Foster Higgins, a New York consulting firm, has found that 28 percent of the plans it surveys now permit employees to move their money around daily. More and more employers let their workers move their money around at least every 90 days. Massachusetts Mutual has found that 85 percent of companies with 401(k)s plans allow changes or transfers at least every 120 days.

At the other extreme from companies that offer limited choices are companies that almost allow the sky to be the limit.

Thanks to State Street Brokerage Services in Boston, employees of Pepsico and other companies can choose among more than 1,200 mutual funds—along with any number of individual stocks and bonds.

Says State Street vice president Joseph Eck, "There'll be a number of people walking around with $100,000 balances in their defined contribution programs, and they won't be satisfied with four investment options. Participants are demanding more and more choice."

To discourage investors from gambling rather than investing, State Street urges individuals to invest no more than half their plan assets in a brokerage account. Still, Eck says that "We assume people who use brokers are astute." Most of them, in fact, prefer mutual funds to individual stocks.

7

HOW GOOD IS YOUR
401(K) PLAN?

A simple way to evaluate your plan is to ask: How much does your company match of every dollar you contribute? And at what point does the matching stop?

Three Key Numbers

It's easy to get confused by the key numbers in 401(k) plans.

First: *What amount can you contribute to a 401(k) plan?* Your employer might set a limit of 10 percent of your salary. So, if you're earning $30,000, you can contribute up to $3,000.

Next: *What does your company match of every dollar you contribute?* 25 cents? 50 cents? A dollar? More? Let's say that it's 75 cents. So, if you contribute $1,000, your employer would contribute $750—75 cents on the dollar.

Finally: *Up to what percentage of your salary would your employer match?* Let's say that it's 5 percent. Your salary is $30,000, so your employer would match up to $1,500 (5% times $30,000). That means you would receive a maximum of $1,150 (75% of $1,500) if you contributed at least $1,500.

Here's the formula:

Maximum you might receive = company match per $1 you contribute × percentage of salary your company matches (. . . provided that this is less than the percentage of your salary that you are allowed to contribute that will be tax-deferred).

A survey by *Worth* magazine (January 1994) of the fifty largest plans found that one company, Abbott Laboratories, matches $2.96 on the dollar, and another, Texaco, matches $2 on the dollar. Some companies made no matching contributions at all. Other companies matched anywhere from $0.24 to $1.33, with $1 being common.

Some companies (Boeing, for example) matched 8 percent of compensation. Those that made no contributions also had no percentage of matching, of course. Matches of 5 percent, 6 percent, and 7 percent of compensation were common.

The top-rated company in *Worth*'s survey, Conoco, matched 6 percent of contributions dollar for dollar. If you contributed $3,000, Conoco would have given you $3,000. (The ratings depended on the total return that investments would have given to typical employees.)

Another way to judge a 401(k) plan: *Does it have a good variety of choices*? Three choices are common: stocks, guaranteed investment contracts, money market funds. Five or six is also fairly common, and might include a fixed-income fund and a balanced fund.

A survey in 1992 by Buck Consultants of companies with 401(k) plans found that 10 percent offer one to three investment choices; 25 percent offer three; 48 percent offer four or five; 15 percent offer six to ten; and 1 percent offer over ten

Some employers give their workers a cornucopia of choices. The World Wildlife Fund in Washington, D.C., offers forty-five choices in its 403(b) plan.

Beyond stocks, GICs (see Key 30), a fixed-income fund, and balanced funds, you might want an index fund for stocks, an index fund for bonds, a fund that invests in foreign stocks, a fund that invests in foreign bonds, a fund that invests in small U.S. companies, and various types of fixed-income funds (investment grade corporate bonds, low-rated bonds, mortgage-back securities).

A fairly new option is an asset-allocation or lifestyle fund, which does it all—one-stop shopping. This is a sensible choice for employers to offer to unsophisticated investors.

At Honeywell, workers can choose a fund (Stocks Plus) that invests 50 percent in U.S. stocks, 15 percent in foreign stocks, 30 percent in bonds, and 5 percent in Treasury bills—sort of a generic portfolio. Employees close to retirement can move over to Bonds Plus, a fund with 60 percent in bonds, 30 percent in U.S. stocks, and 10 percent in Treasury bills.

IBM offers a Balanced Asset Fund, a sort of "fund of funds." It combined five other IBM funds offered to employees: 40 percent in an index of large companies (like the Standard & Poor's 500 Stock Index), 30 percent in a fixed-income fund, and 10 percent each in a small-company index fund, an international stock fund, and a U.S. government securities fund. IBM recommends the fund, which has 60 percent in stocks, to people in the middle of their careers.

Worth magazine rated large companies on their investment options, giving Marathon Oil, Texaco, 3M, State Farm, Unisys, and IBM high grades.

How well the companies' 401(k) plans have performed financially was *Worth*'s chief criterion in ranking the plans. The rating was based on a three-year time period for certain higher-paid employees who put 75 percent into stocks and 25 percent into fixed-income securities. IBM came in last.

But *Worth*'s rating system was flawed. The returns were not "risk-adjusted": volatile funds were not penalized, funds that were stable were not rewarded. So the ratings were only half of the story. Risk-adjusted ratings are more suitable for conservative investors than are simple "total return" ratings.

With your own 401(k) plan, check how each fund has performed in the past—if it's not a new fund. Or see if you can find the portfolio manager's track record. Go to a library and inspect *Morningstar Mutual Funds* or *Value Line Mutual Funds*, two newsletters, or issues of *Business Week*, *Money*, or *Forbes* that rate mutual funds.

In evaluating any funds, stress the three and five-year records, but look at the one-year and ten-year records, too.

For list of top mutual fund families, see Key 24.

Worth did provide a simple guide to evaluating your company's own plan: check how much you can contribute as a percentage of your salary; what your employer will match for every $1 of your own contribution; what percentage of your salary your employer will match; and the number of investment options.

How Does Your Plan Compare?

	Low	High	Average
Maximum contribution	7%	20%	13.5%
Employer Dollar Matching	$ 0	$2.96	$0.76
Maximum salary matched	0%	10%	*5.2%
Number of investment options	2	17	5

*Not identified among top 50
Source: *Worth* magazine, January 1994.

Another way to evaluate 401(k) plans: *Do the employers give their workers guidance?* Some companies provide newsletters, seminars, lectures, and even suggested asset-allocation models (how much you should have in stocks, bonds, and cash, depending on your age, prosperity, and goals).

IBM employees can figure out how much to contribute by using a computer program that considers their salary, possible investment returns, possible inflation rates, expected Social Security benefits, and even income from their spouses' pension plans.

Some employers allow their workers to change their allocations every day; others permit it only four times a year. No one wants to encourage workers to switch in and out—that's only for daring, sophisticated investors. On the other hand, being able to switch only every four months might be frustrating if the stock market began declining steadily on bad economic news, or if interest rates starting climbing as inflation seemed to be roaring back.

By the same token, there's a dispute over how often assets inside 401(k) plans should be valued. Monthly? Daily? The trend is toward daily.

There's no easy decision, but erring on the side of greater freedom usually seems to be the better idea.

In short, the most desirable 401(k) plans have
- generous employer matching contributions, both as to the dollar amount matched per dollar of worker contribution and to the limit;

- a healthy variety of choices, including foreign stocks and bonds and an asset-allocation fund;
- money managers—and funds—with good track records;
- a worker's ability to switch investments more than once every quarter; and
- company-sponsored guidance, via newsletters or lectures.

What Five Giant Employers Offer

Company	Highest Worker Contribution	Options	Employer Match
GM	15%	GM stock EDS stock Hughes stock U.S. Savings Bonds Stock fund Bond fund GIC	25 cents per $1 to 6% of salary
Exxon	14%	Exxon stock Stock fund Fixed-income fund	$1 per $1 to 6% of salary—7% if match is in Exxon stock
Ford	15%	Ford stock Stock fund Bond fund Money market fund GIC	50 cents per $1 to 5% of salary
IBM	9%	4 stock funds Bond fund Money market fund Fixed-income fund Asset-allocation fund	30 cents per $1 to 5% of salary
GE	15%	GE stock U.S. Savings Bonds Stock fund Bond fund Money market fund Fixed-income fund	50 cents per $1 to 6% of salary (7% after 3 years)

8

THE DOWNSIDE
OF 401(K) PLANS

There's a case against 401(k) plans: ordinary investors may not know how to invest in them properly. They may do dumb things—including not investing in them in the first place. They may invest in them so unwisely that they wind up losing money, either directly or just to inflation.

A 401(k) plan requires that you take charge of your own investments, and that means—unfortunately—that some unlucky people are going to be blown out of the water.

A survey by John Hancock Financial Services has found that almost half of 401(k) participants thought that money market funds contained stocks and bonds.

Only 25 percent knew that the best time to buy bonds is when interest rates are declining. (When rates decline, existing bonds are worth more.)

Pension managers tend to be much more sophisticated than participants in 401(k) plans. Here's how the two were investing in 1992:

In Praise of Pros

	Pension managers	Individuals
Amount in cash	4.6%	7.8%
Amount in GICs	0.8	31.0
Amount in stocks	50	50*
Foreign stocks, bonds	10.1	1.0

*31.1% in employers' stock.

The critics don't argue that employees should avoid investing in 401(k) plans altogether. They argue that employees must be encouraged to learn more about them—through reading whatever literature a company may provide or reading books like this one.

At one time, employees didn't have to invest voluntarily;they didn't have to manage their own money. Defined-benefit plans ruled the roost. Now these traditional plans are being replaced by defined-contribution plans, particularly among small companies. And John Doe and Jane Roe must now make vital investment decisions on their own.

The percentage of workers covered by defined-benefit plans has dropped from about 48 percent to 39 percent, according to the *Social Security Bulletin* (October 1989). The number of 401(k) plans rose from 17,303 in 1984, covering 7.5 million workers, to 83,301 in 1989, covering 17.3 million people, according to the Employee Benefit Research Institute.

The basic questions are: 1. Do enough people opt to make 401(k) contributions? 2. Do they invest enough? 3. Do they invest wisely?

The answers are not encouraging.

"If you look at people with under $25,000, the percentage participating is very low," reports Cindy Hounsell, director of the Women's Pension Project at the Pension Rights Center in Washington.

A survey, by KPMG Peat Marwick, found that while most 401(k) plans permit employees to put away up to 13 percent of their income, the employees on average contributed no more than 5 percent.

Another problem is that when people do save, they invest too conservatively—they don't put enough into stocks. They put the bulk of their money into government bond funds or guaranteed investment contracts.

This might be okay if these investors had a lot of their savings outside their pension plans in the stock market. But they don't. Their pension money constitutes most of what they have.

"It's a very well-documented phenomenon that most people, when they control their own portfolio decisions, invest extraordinarily conservatively," Princeton's Bernheim says. "To be investing almost exclusively in the safest asset available means that these people will get much lower returns than if their pension portfolio were professionally managed."

Investing wisely is not easy. Hounsell, a pension expert,

27

confesses that her own IRAs haven't done very well in the ten years she's had them.

CQ Researcher quotes a middle-manager at a large corporation as saying, "Many of my company's employees have entry-level jobs, limited proficiency in English, and minimal education. I have no idea how a person holding a $5-an-hour job is supposed to make those kinds of [investment] decisions."

An Education Department study, mentioned by Bernheim, showed that, among people aged twenty-one to twenty-five, only 44 percent of whites, 20 percent of Hispanics, and 8 percent of blacks could accurately determine how much change they were owed from the purchase of a restaurant meal consisting of two items.

Concludes Bernheim: "It therefore seems highly improbable that most individuals have mastered more advanced concepts such as compound interest, risk-return tradeoffs, inflation adjustments. . . . Most individuals have at best a primitive understanding of the relations between their financial choices and economic outcomes; they are poorly equipped to evaluate economic opportunities and vulnerabilities."

Summing up, Bernheim says: "We have this peculiar situation now. To a greater and greater extent, people are placing the responsibility for saving on their employers by relying primarily on their pensions and Social Security rather than on personal saving. At the same time, the employers are pushing the responsibility back to them by saying, 'You guys have got to make more decisions.' But those are decisions that workers are not prepared to make, and no one's telling them how. In the end, no one takes responsibility, and the investment decisions are made poorly."

What Investors Want

A survey by J. P. Morgan found that employees may not be so unsophisticated as some skeptics believe. Here's what they wanted in a 401(k) plan:

- balanced funds (stocks and bonds) as an investment option
- bond funds and not just GICs
- active management rather than passive (an index fund is passive)
- frequent valuation of their assets

Just from their names, some of these funds, goals are obvious. The goal of aggressive growth funds may not be. They are the most daring, buying stocks of companies on a tear or of companies that almost everyone else is afraid to go near. As you might guess, aggressive growth funds have the highest price-earnings ratios among domestic funds.

Asset allocation funds either keep a predetermined amount of their money in certain investments—stocks, bonds, cash—or shift their assets among such investments, depending on the managers' assessments of the investment climate.

Balanced funds are a combination of stocks and bonds, usually tilted toward stocks, typically 60 percent/40 percent. Funds tilted toward bonds are income funds. Vanguard/ Wellington is a balanced fund; Vanguard/Wellesley Income is an income fund. An equity-income fund invests mostly in relatively high-paying stocks.

Small company funds have the lowest average yields; precious metals have the lowest average yields among the specialty stock funds. Equity-income funds and utility funds have the highest yields.

There are also nine investment styles that managers of stock funds may practice. Three depend upon the size of the companies that the funds invest in: small, medium, or large. Another three depend on what kinds of stocks the funds go after: undervalued (called value) stocks, growth stocks, or a blend of growth and value.

Funds that try to invest in undervalued stocks may be especially suitable for investors who are:
- approaching retirement and who prefer conservative stock investments
- taking distributions from a retirement plan and seeking current dividend income for living expenses (underpriced stocks typically pay higher dividends)
- holding stock funds in tax-deferred plans, where dividends escape current taxation.

Undervalued stocks tend to have low price-earnings ratios and low ratios of prices to book value.

Funds that invest in growing companies may be especially suitable for

- young investors setting aside money for retirement
- prosperous, sophisticated investors who can tolerate somewhat higher volatility
- investors with long time-horizons, who can wait out steep market declines.

Growth stocks tend to have high price-earnings ratios and high ratios of price to book value. Their earnings also tend to accelerate much faster than the earnings of value stocks.

Certain families of funds are famous for seeking under-valued stocks: the Mutual Series group in Short Hills, N.J., for instance, and Neuberger & Berman in New York City. Twentieth Century funds in Kansas City and Value Line in New York City are noted for investing in growth stocks.

26

BALANCED FUNDS

If you have a limited amount of choices in your 401(k) plan and you want some exposure to stocks, consider a balanced fund. Such a fund may be the single best kind of fund to own in a 401(k) plan, especially for fairly unsophisticated investors.

A balanced fund is typically 60 percent invested in stocks and 40 percent in bonds. Actually, those percentages are rough, most balanced funds keeping some money in cash and varying the percentages between stocks and bonds. Many balanced funds have 50 percent in stocks and 50 percent in bonds. But a fund that has more bonds than stocks becomes an income fund. And a fund that has more than 60 percent in stocks is on its way to becoming an equity-income fund.

Here are some of the benefits of a balanced fund:

- You have a healthy exposure to the stock market, typically in conservative stocks.
- Your fund won't be as volatile as the stock market—in part because of your hefty dose of bonds and in part because of the conservatism of the stock-market component.
- You are less likely to lose money in a balanced fund than you are in the stock market. One reason is that stocks and bonds go in different directions about half of the time. And if the stock market goes sideways, you should have some income from the bonds you own (along with the stock dividends).
- A balanced fund will probably practice a passive form of market-timing. If the stock market goes up and now constitutes more than 60 percent of the holdings, stocks will be sold and more money shifted into bonds. If bonds have soared and stocks have languished or fallen, the bond holdings will be cut back, and more money put into stocks. If both bonds and stocks have fallen or climbed in

equal measure, the manager may stand still.

- The fund's managers may have the option to practice a slightly more aggressive form of market-timing, moving from 60 percent in stocks, say, to 50 percent. But this is fairly modest—and modest forms of market-timing are typically the most successful.

In the long run, you would surely make more money in an all-stock fund. But in the long run, you may have been so terrified by a sudden decline in the stock market that you moved into money market funds or guaranteed investment contracts. A balanced fund may not do so well as a stock fund, but it won't be so volatile, either.

Even so, over the ten-year period ending in 1993, balanced funds acquitted themselves with honor, thanks to the unusually strong performance of bonds. Among diversified funds, they were beaten only by foreign stock funds. (See listing in Key 25.)

27

FOREIGN STOCK FUNDS

Not many pension plans offer foreign-stock funds, but if your 401(k) plan does allow you to invest in a foreign (or international) stock fund, you should probably spring for the opportunity.

The U.S. stock market is not always the best-performing market; U.S. stock funds are not always the best-performing stock funds. From 1983 through 1992, the U.S. market's return actually was among the top five countries only twice. Hong Kong was on top twice, and was second once. Norway made the list four times.

The Five Strongest Major Stock Markets, 1983–1992

1983	Total Return
Norway	82.2%
Denmark	58.4
Australia	56.1
Sweden	50.3
Netherlands	38.4

1984	
Hong Kong	47.0%
Spain	41.7
Japan	17.1
Belgium	13.3
Netherlands	11.5

1985	
Austria	177.3%
Germany	136.5
Italy	133.8
Switzerland	107.5
France	83.2

1986	
Spain	123.1%
Italy	109.4

Japan	99.7
Belgium	80.6
France	79.1

1987

Japan	43.2%
Spain	37.9
United Kingdom	35.1
Canada	14.7
Denmark	14.0

1988

Belgium	53.6%
Denmark	52.7
Sweden	48.3
France	37.9
Norway	42.4

1989

Austria	104.8%
Germany	47.1
Norway	46.1
Denmark	44.7
Singapore/Malaysia	42.3

1990

United Kingdom	10.3%
Hong Kong	9.2
Austria	6.3
Norway	0.6
Denmark	−0.9

1991

Hong Kong	42.8%
Australia	29.1
U.S.	**27.2**
Singapore/Malaysia	22.7
France	15.8

1992

Hong Kong	32.3%
Switzerland	18.1
U.S.	**7.4**
Singapore/Malaysia	6.3
Netherlands	3.4

Source: Hotchkis and Wiley International

Making more money is an obvious reason to consider investing abroad. Another reason is to add stability to your portfolio. Foreign stock funds don't march in step with U.S. stock funds, and in any year that U.S. funds suffer, foreign funds may soar. Here's a comparison of the total returns of foreign stock funds with Vanguard Index 500-Series, a mirror of the U.S. stock market:

Total Returns

Year	Vanguard Index 500	Foreign Stock Funds
1983	21.29%	27.73%
1984	6.21	−4.71
1985	31.23	44.44
1986	18.06	44.49
1987	4.71	8.24
1988	16.22	17.43
1989	31.37	21.98
1990	−3.33	−12.07
1991	30.22	12.47
1992	7.42	−4.55
1993	9.89	31.60

Source: Mutual Fund Sourcebook, Morningstar, Inc.

Since 1983, foreign funds lost money in three years; in two of those years, the U.S. market had a positive total return. The U.S. market lost money in only one year, 1990, but that was a year in which foreign funds also lost money.

But let's compare the total returns only in years in which foreign funds did splendidly: in 1985, foreign funds beat the U.S. market by 13.21 percentage points; in 1986, by 26.43 percentage points; in 1993, by 12.44 percentage points. The biggest one-year difference between the U.S. market and foreign markets came in 1991, when the difference in favor of the U.S. market was 17.75 percentage points.

Three warnings about foreign funds:

There's a big difference between them. Some have been top performers, some have been miserable performers.

Following are the top five performers for the five-year period ending in October 31, 1993—and the bottom five performers. Compare their total returns.

The Top Five Foreign Stock Funds (5 Years)

Fund	Average Return
Smith Barney International Equity A	17.39%
GAM International	17.19
Harbor International	16.53
Europacific Growth	15.05
Templeton Foreign	14.44

The Bottom Five Foreign Stock Funds (5 Years)

Fund	Average Return
Quantitative Boston Foreign Growth & Income	1.77
Alliance Global Canadian	2.44
Boston Company International Retail	2.96
Mackenzie Canada	3.11
Keystone International	3.64

If you go even further down the list of poorest performers over five years, you encounter some well-known names: INVESCO, Colonial, Flag Investors.

Clearly, you must look for an international fund with a good track record. Think twice before putting money into a totally new fund, even if it's from a well-respected family—like INVESCO. (Funds open to retirement-plan investors aren't the same as the funds open to general investors, but a retirement-plan fund may be modeled on an existing fund.)

Beware of subvarieties of foreign funds.

There are funds that specialize in investing in European companies, in small European companies, in Southeast Asia, in Pacific companies, in developing markets, in Latin America, in Hong Kong, in Japan, in Japanese small companies, in Canadian companies, in the United Kingdom, Italy, Israel, the Netherlands, Spain, and so forth. There are also global or world funds, which invest both domestically and abroad.

You would probably do best sticking with broadly based foreign funds and thus being more diversified.

Limit your investments in foreign funds.

With foreign stocks, you face extra hazards. One is currency risk. If the U.S. dollar becomes stronger, your foreign stocks may be worth less in U.S. dollars. Another hazard is political risk. Few countries in the world are as stable as the

United States. Then there's economic risk, especially with the developing countries. There's also financial risk: in a few foreign countries, the accounting and ethical standards are not at the level of the United States.

You should probably keep only 10 percent to 30 percent of your assets in foreign stocks—the percentage depending to a large extent on which countries you're investing in, large and stable or small and unstable.

Less than twenty years ago, the U.S. stock markets accounted for more than 60 percent of the value of the world stock markets. Now it's only around 37 percent. While the U.S. market has grown, so have the markets of other countries.

World Stock Market Values

U.S.	37%
Japan	29
United Kingdom	10
France	4
Germany	4
Hong Kong	3
Switzerland	3
Canada	2
Others	9*

*Total is 101 percent because of rounding.
Source: Morgan Stanley Capital International

28

INDEX FUNDS

To find out whether Americans like a new television show or a candidate for President, a pollster will ask 1,000 or more representative Americans from all over the country for their views.

To find out what the "stock market" did yesterday, or all year, or during the past 60 years, a market analyst may check out a list of just 30 enormous companies (the Dow Jones Industral Average)—although there are 7,000 stocks that the public can buy or sell.

An index is typically a mirror of an investment market. It's a sampling of the stocks in various markets in the United States, or in the Far East, or in Europe. Or it's a sampling of the bonds in various fixed-income markets.

There are also indexes of small-company stocks, of transportation stocks, of health-care stocks, of real estate investment trusts, of gold stocks . . . the list goes on and on.

Index funds can also mirror investment styles. There's an index of undervalued stocks, an index of growth stocks.

Indexes are used to take the pulse of a market, to check what it has done—without someone's having to check out every single component of the market.

But indexes have another use. If you buy all the stocks or bonds in the index (or a sampling), your portfolio should do as well as the index—and the market. And you can actually buy an index—through an index mutual fund that mirrors a particular kind of market.

Index funds are especially suitable for
- conservative investors—such as those nearing retirement;
- beginning investors—because index funds are easy to understand and relatively safe.

Index funds have clear advantages:
- They are inexpensive to run. You don't have to pay a port-

folio manager a lot of money to decide which stocks or bonds to buy. You don't have to pay brokers high amounts of commissions to buy and sell securities. (Indexes don't change their securities very often simply because the components of the index remain there a long time.)

- They are well diversified. While many mutual funds own a variety of securities, they may not own as many securities in different industries as an index. Many portfolio managers, in order to outperform an index, will emphasize certain sectors of the economy—and thus at times may be underweighted in, say, utilities or health-care stocks or financials. But while portfolio managers may beat an index this way, chances are also good that they will have erred—and will underperform the index.
- They do rather well. Because of their economy and their wide diversification, they don't just do average. They do better than average. The oldest index fund open to the general public, dating back to 1974, is Vanguard Index 500 Series. *Morningstar* rates its record, taking into consideration its total return and its volatility, as four stars— "above average."

Stuart P. Kaye, a pension fund manager, has adduced other reasons why index funds tend to do well:

- Actively managed funds occasionally lose their portfolio managers, who retire, go elsewhere, or die. The new manager may not be as good, or may simply follow a different strategy, which requires an expensive change in the fund's holdings.
- The assets that the manager handles may climb—and managing a large fund is a rather different animal from handling a small or intermediate-sized fund,
- Investment styles—growth versus value—go in and out of fashion. This means that managers may do exceptionally well when their style is in favor, exceptionally poorly when their style is out of favor. An index fund is a blend of styles, holding as it does undervalued stocks as well as the stock of growing companies.

But index funds have disadvantages, too.

- They don't do spectacularly well. They are never among

the very top performers in any year.

- They are relatively volatile. A mutual fund modeled after the S&P 500, for example, will bob up and down more than a fund that also owns bonds—a "balanced" fund. (See Key 26.)
- They tend to give short shrift to small-company stocks. Most index stock funds are modeled after the Standard & Poor's 500 Stock Index or the Dow Jones Industrial Average, two indexes that are sharply tilted toward big-company stocks. Few index funds emulate an index of small-company stocks, like the Russell 2000 or Wilshire 4500, or even better-diversified indexes, like the Value Line Composite or the Wilshire 5000. (The Wilshire 5000 is the Wilshire 4500 with the 500 stocks in the Standard & Poor's index.) And small-company stocks tend to do better than large-company stocks.

The S&P 500, by the way, is a better mirror of the stock market than the Dow because its stocks are "weighted" by their "capitalization"—the number of their shares outstanding times their prices. The Dow Jones Industrial Average really is an average, and it tends to be dominated by stocks with high prices.

29

FIXED-INCOME FUNDS

Inside a retirement plan, your first goal should be to have conservative fixed-income investments: those with short maturities and high credit ratings. Short or intermediate-term Treasuries would be ideal; after that, short or intermediate-term investment grade (high rated) corporate bonds.

As you grow more prosperous and sophisticated, you should consider spreading out—into longer maturities, lower investment grades, and even into such exotic fare as convertible securities and foreign bonds. As you approach retirement, move to shorter maturities and higher quality.

"Short term" generally means up to five years; intermediate means five to ten years; long-term means over ten years. As mentioned, the further out you go into the future, the greater the interest rates you receive but also the greater the risk.

Make sure that you know what the credit rating is on the bonds inside any fixed-income funds that you buy. You may not want to be buying junk bonds instead of investment grade bonds.

Make sure you know the average maturity (or duration) of the bonds inside any fixed-income funds that you buy. Otherwise, you may own long-term bonds when your preference would have been for safer short-term bonds.

Often an investor cannot tell exactly what he or she is buying from the name of a fixed-income fund—what the average maturity of a bond fund is, or what the average credit rating is.

Sometimes you cannot even know what a fixed-income fund is buying. Some funds that call themselves "government" funds own a lot of mortgage-backed securities, and they are not quite the same as Treasuries.

On the following page is how Morningstar Inc. separates the various types of fixed-income funds you might find inside a pension plan, and their ten-year annualized total returns to 1994. The riskier funds, like junk bond funds, have in general returned more than the conservative funds, like Treasury funds.

Fixed Income Funds

Fund Type	Total Return
Specialty bond	11.18
Convertible bond	10.93
High yield ("junk")	11.21
World bond	11.17
Corporate bond	11.15
General	11.57
High quality	10.77
Short-term world income	−8.52*
Government bond	10.11
Adjustable rate mortgages	7.73*
General	9.96
Mortgages	10.25
Treasuries	10.61
Municipal bond	10.03
National	10.06
Single state	9.66

*Five years.

30

GUARANTEED INVESTMENT CONTRACTS

Sophisticated investors tend to heap scorn on GICs. "They are often riddled with high fees, the fixed-rates aren't inflation-proof, and the government doesn't provide a security net," writes Lee Rosenberg, a Certified Financial Planner. As for the word "guaranteed," he notes: "A guarantee from some insurance companies and banks today may be one step above a handshake." (He has in mind, of course, the financial problems of two giant insurance companies, Mutual Benefit and Executive Life.)

Other critics contend that too many Americans put too much of their retirement money into their GICs, meanwhile avoiding the stock market, which is where the real profits lie. But a case can be made for GICs:

- They pay adequately—usually more than money market funds and certificates of deposit, and closer to short-term bonds.
- They're not so conservative as money-market funds.
- If someone is unsophisticated and might become anxious and worried because of (perhaps only temporary) losses in equity (stock) or balanced (stock and bond) funds, GICs are a good, safe way for that person to get started.
- GICs can help shield a portfolio against too much volatility from the stock market, volatility that could panic an investor into foolishly selling into a down market. If your portfolio is 50 percent into equities and 50 percent into GICs, you probably won't experience wild swings in your assets.

Just how much you should invest in GICs depends on your age, your sophistication, your overall wealth, and so forth. (See Key 33.)

The worst accusation that can be made against GICs is that the word "guaranteed" in their names can be misleading. They certainly are not backed by the full faith and credit of the U.S. government, the way a bank account is (up to $100,000). Typically GICs are "guaranteed" only by the insurance companies issuing them, and if an insurance company goes belly-up, your GIC may be carried off to sea, too. That's why you or your trustee should periodically check the financial soundness of the company issuing the GIC.

GICs are like bank certificates of deposit. They pay regular interest for one year to five years. When the term of the GIC ends, it can be renewed at going interest rates. Like CDs, the value of a GIC doesn't bob up and down, the way stock and bond prices fluctuate.

Unlike CDs, GICs are not federally insured by the Federal Deposit Insurance Corporation.

GICs may have other names—stable value fund, fixed-income fund, capital-preservation fund, guaranteed fund.

How safe are your employer's GICs? One way of telling is to check how many companies are issuing the GICs: four to six different insurors or banks are desirable, not just a few. Then check into the insurers' credit ratings. Look for those rated "AAA" or "AA" by Standard & Poor's, Moody's, or Duff & Phelps. Ask your plan sponsor to tell you the ratings of the insurance companies issuing your GICs.

While banks cannot issue GICs, they can and do issue BICs—bank investment contracts. Unlike GICs, these are insured by the federal government up to $100,000 per account.

In the future, GICs may become more sophisticated instruments, actively managed to reap higher rewards from a variety of fixed-income vehicles.

31

WHICH FUNDS TO BUY

The mutual funds in your 401(k) portfolio should be varied. They should cover enough different kinds of markets and different kinds of strategies so that, even if one of them fails you shamefully, the others will help carry you along to victory.

A panel of distinguished mutual fund investment authorities was asked: How many funds should someone own? The consensus: five to eight. (*The Ultimate Mutual Fund Guide*, Probus Publishing, 1993, Boroson.)

What general types of funds should you avoid? The authorities' answer was sector or specialty funds—although some of the experts would make an exception for such broad sectors as technology funds, health-care funds, and real estate.

Here are the types of funds that these experts believe that investors should have in their portfolios:

- growth funds
- small capitalization funds
- growth and income funds
- international funds
- equity-income funds
- fixed-income funds

The panelists were somewhat skeptical about balanced funds, aggressive growth funds, and global funds (U.S. and foreign stocks). They were even more dubious about flexible or "asset allocation funds."

The sentiment of some of the experts was that certain types of funds don't have clear-cut guidelines, "equity income" being an example. In other words, the name doesn't convey much about the fund.

As for growth and income funds and balanced funds, the thinking of some experts was that investors should concentrate on individual funds—growth funds, income funds, stock funds, fixed-income funds, and not mix the colors on their palette.

Beyond the types of funds, investors should also check into the funds' strategies. It would be ideal to own both value and growth stock funds, for instance; funds that invest in big-company stocks and small-company stocks; and a variety of fixed-income funds, including high-yield bonds and foreign bonds.

32

SETTING UP A PORTFOLIO

What your 401(k) portfolio looks like—how much you have in stocks, bonds, and cash—is your asset allocation. The decision about how to divide up your money is not to be taken lightly. (See Key 33.)

A famous study (by Brinson, Hood, and Beebower, 1986) checked the performance results from ninety-one large U.S. pension plans between 1974 and 1983. The investigators examined how three factor determined portfolio results:

- asset allocation;
- market-timing; and
- choosing stocks.

What they found was that the first factor—how much the pension was invested in stocks, bonds, or cash—was by far the most important. In fact, they found that 94 percent of the variations in the portfolios' results was due to the asset allocations.

One can fault this experiment on various grounds. The asset mix may actually be influenced by market-timing decisions. You will have more in stocks when you think they are undervalued than when you consider them overvalued.

Also, presumably the higher a portfolio's exposure to the stock market, the better it will normally perform over any extended period of time. But if you must sell your holdings for any reason while the stock market is depressed, your portfolio will take a severe hit. And if—unlike those pension managers—you are not a professional and you are easily spooked by stock market ups and downs and ready to pull out at every small hiccup, your asset mix should be very much different—more conservative.

In later Keys, we shall present some asset allocation models—from conservative to aggressive.

There is no definitive asset allocation model. With 401(k)

plans, some of which offer only a few alternatives, you may not even be able to follow many of the more sophisticated asset-allocation models, such as those that call for foreign investments or even for gold-mining stocks.

Besides, even asset allocation models change over time. Older models allocate a lot to cash (money market funds). Newer models have tilted toward foreign stock funds.

Later Keys will describe conservative models, aggressive models, simple models and complex models. You should choose a model that fits your age, needs, and desires, and stick with it unless your circumstances change.

33

ASSET ALLOCATION

Your first big decision was whether to join your employer's 401(k) plan. Your next big decisions are: how much to contribute and where to invest your money.

The way you invest your money—whether in stocks, fixed-income investments (like GICs), or money-market funds—is known as "asset allocation."

A sort of generic asset-allocation model is: 10 percent in cash (money market funds), 60 percent in stocks, and 30 percent in fixed-income investments.

The cash is there (1) to reduce your portfolio's volatility, (2) to provide you with opportunity money (if stocks fall off the table, you want to have some cash to buy in), and (3) to let you take advantage of climbing short-term interest rates if inflation comes galumphing back. (See Key 23.)

Fixed-income investments also serve to reduce the volatility of your portfolio. They also give you a regular, predictable return on your money, a return that's typically better than money market funds and Treasury bills give you. Over the years, bonds have done a little better than the inflation rate.

Stocks are where the big money is, which is why the ordinary investor may want to have some retirement money there at all times.

The trouble with stocks—and with the stock market—is that they can be volatile. The market lost 48 percent of its value in 1973 and 1974; it wasn't until 1977 that an investor in 1972 would have recouped his money. If you needed cash during that period, you might have been forced to sell some of your stocks—at a loss.

That's one reason you should limit your exposure to the stock market: you might need money, and the market may be underpriced just then. Another reason: if the market went down and remained down for a few years, more and more investors would become discouraged—and sell. That would drive down prices even more.

Third reason: you might not be able to wait out a decline in the stock market. You're retiring next year, at sixty-five, say. The market suddenly goes into a nosedive—and remains depressed for seven years. Could you wait to get your money? Would you have the patience? The courage?

The percentage of your retirement money that should be in a well-diversified portfolio of stocks depends upon

1. your age (the younger you are, the more you might have in stocks—because, not needing the money, you can wait out declines);
2. your overall prosperity (you probably can wait out any decline before you need money to live on); and
3. your risk tolerance or investment sophistication (in other words, the less likely you are to panic and sell when the market retreats). See Key 16.

There is no single "right" asset allocation for everyone. You have a wide lattitude of models to choose from.

Here's a worksheet to figure out your current asset allocation:

Asset Allocation Worksheet

CASH
Savings accounts	——	
Money market funds	——	
Treasury bills	——	
Subtotal		$ —— (A)
Percent of total (A/D)	—— %	

BONDS
Corporate High Quality	——	
Corporate High Yield	——	
Municipal	——	
Foreign	——	
Treasuries, Savings Bonds	——	
Other	——	
Subtotal		$ —— (B)
Percent of total (B/D)	—— %	

STOCKS
U.S. Large Cap	——	
U.S. Mid Cap	——	
U.S. Small Cap	——	
Foreign	——	
Subtotal		$ —— (C)
Percent of total (C/D)	—— %	
Total Savings and Investments		$ —— (D)

34

CONSERVATIVE MODELS

Here's a quick and dirty rule: A conservative asset-allocation model is one that recommends that investors over sixty (or close to retirement) have less than 50 percent of their assets in the stock market.

This conservative model comes from the American Association of Individual Investors in Chicago:

Risk Tolerance	Stocks	Bonds	Cash
Five years or more from retirement			
Conservative	40%	30%	30%
Aggressive	60%	30%	10%
Close to retirement			
Conservative	20%	50%	30%
Aggressive	40%	40%	20%
At retirement			
Conservative	0%	50%	50%
Aggressive	20%	50%	30%

This happens to be one of the author's favorites. It reflects the conservatism of most investors. And it is derived from history—how much you can lose in stocks or bonds in any year. Other models seem to ignore the 1929 Depression, their creators apparently feeling that such an economic catastrophe is extremely unlikely to recur.

Now look at this model, also conservative, from the Capital Consulting Group in Livonia, Michigan:

For Conservative Investors

Age	Stocks	Bonds	Bills
20–30	60%	20%	20%
30–40	50	25	25
40–50	40	30	30

Age	Stocks	Bonds	Bills
50–60	30	35	35
60–70	20	40	40
70	+10	45	45

For Moderate Investors

Age	Stocks	Bonds	Bills
20–30	70%	15%	15%
30–40	60	20	20
40–50	50	25	25
50–60	40	30	30
60–70	30	35	35
70+	20	40	40

For Aggressive Investors

Age	Stocks	Bonds	Bills
20–30	80%	10%	10%
30–40	70	15	15
40–50	60	20	20
50–60	50	25	25
60–70	40	30	30
70+	30	35	35

To compare the two models, let's assume, in the first, that "five or more years from retirement" means age fifty to fifty-five; "close to retirement" means fifty-five to sixty; and "at retirement" means sixty to sixty-five.

So, according to the AAII, someone of fifty who is conservative might be 40 percent in stocks, 30 percent in bonds; someone of fifty who is aggressive might be 60 percent in stocks, 30 percent in bonds.

According to the Capital Consulting Group, a conservative person of fifty might be 30 percent in stocks, 35 percent in bonds; an aggressive fifty-year-old might be 50 percent in stocks, 25 percent in bonds. Thus, Capital Consulting's model is more conservative.

Someone aged fifty-five who is conservative, according to the AAII, might be 20 percent in stocks, 50 percent in bonds; someone aggressive might be 40 percent in stocks, 40 percent in bonds.

Capital Consulting Group suggests that a conservative fifty-five-year-old be 30 percent in stocks, 35 percent in bonds. An aggressive investor might be 50 percent in stocks,

25 percent in bonds. Here, Capital Consulting's model is more aggressive.

Someone aged sixty or more, the AAII suggests, might have nothing in stocks if conservative, and 50 percent in bonds; if aggressive, 20 percent in stocks, 50 percent in bonds.

Capital Consulting Group recommends that a conservative sixty-year-old be 30 percent in stocks, 35 percent in bonds. An aggressive investor might be 40 percent in stocks, 30 percent in bonds. Here, Capital Consulting is far more aggressive. But it's still conservative compared with other models described in later Keys.

Recently the Vanguard Group came out with a four-part asset-allocation portfolio.

1. For investors age 20–49, with children up to age 10, it recommended a growth portfolio: 80 percent in stocks, 20 percent in bonds. Historic return (1926–1993): 9.6 percent. Years with a loss (1926–1993): one in four. Average loss: –10 percent. Worst annual loss (1931): –36 percent.

2. For investors 50–59 (children between 11 and 14), it recommended a balanced growth portfolio: 60 percent stocks, 40 percent bonds. Historic return: 8.6 percent. Years with a loss: one in five. Average loss: –9 percent. Worst annual loss: –28 percent.

3. For investors 60–74, it recommended a conservative growth portfolio: 40 percent stocks, 40 percent bonds, 20 percent cash. Historic return: 7.4 percent. Years with a loss: one in five. Average loss: –5 percent. Worst annual loss: –19 percent.

4. For investors 75 and over, it recommended an income portfolio: 20 percent stocks, 60 percent bonds, 20 percent cash. Historic return: 6.2 percent. Years with a loss: one in six. Average loss: –3 percent. Worst annual loss: –12 percent.

35

AGGRESSIVE MODELS

A crude but aggressive asset-allocation guide is: take your age, subtract it from 100, and keep the resulting number (as a percentage) in stocks. If you're thirty, you should be 70 percent in stocks; if you're forty, 60 percent; if fifty, 50 percent; if sixty, 40 percent.

This guide has the virtues of

- simplicity;
- reducing your exposure to the market as you grow older; and
- keeping you modestly in the market in your later years, as you should be.

But this guide is very risky. Not many seventy-year-olds would want to be 30 percent in the stock market—unless they were very wealthy or financially sophisticated, or they were investing not only for themselves but for their younger heirs.

Below is another very aggressive model, recommended by *Worth* magazine (January 1994). Allocations don't change with an investor's age. Everyone, it seems, should be 75 percent in the stock market and have nothing whatsoever in GICs and cash equivalents:

Diversified stocks or mutual funds	50%
Growth stocks or mutual funds	25
Bonds/bond funds	25
GICs	0
Money market accounts	0

Next is a much more complex model, from the brokerage firm of Piper, Jaffray & Hopwood, based in Minneapolis. This model is unusual for these reasons:

- It differentiates between risk-taking and risk-averse couples between ages thirty and forty.

- The model for a risk-averse couple aged thirty to forty is discontinuous with the model for a couple aged fifty to sixty (they are supposed to jump from 25 percent in utilities to 65 percent in stocks, for example); and
- The model for someone aged fifty to sixty is sharply divergent from the one for someone retired aged sixty and over (declining from 65 percent to 20 percent in stocks).

Young Single, 20 to 30

Stocks:	80%	U.S., 50%; foreign, 30%
Bonds:	10%	long-term
Inflation hedges:	5%	gold, real estate
Liquid assets:	5%	

Young Professional Couple, 30 to 40, 1 to 2 Children

Stocks:	65%	U.S., 45% growth; foreign, 20%
Fixed-income:	25%	zero coupon bonds, for college
Inflation hedges:	5%	
Liquid assets:	5%	

Young Working Couple, 30 to 40, 2 Children

Stocks:	35%	U.S. 25%—conservative growth; foreign, 10%
Fixed Income:	40%	laddered maturities
Inflation hedges:	10%	
Liquid assets:	15%	CDs

Early Middle-Aged, 40 to 50, with Teenage or Young Adult Children

Stocks:	25%	utilities
Fixed Income:	45%	1–5 year maturities
Liquid assets:	15%	
Foreign bonds:	10%	
Inflation hedges:	5%	

Pre-Retirement Middle-Aged, 50 to 60

Stocks:	65%	U.S. 40%—conservative to moderately aggressive; foreign stocks: 25%
Fixed income:	25%	laddered maturities
Liquid assets:	5%	
Inflation hedges:	5%	

Retiree, 60+ Years Old

Stocks: U.S.	20%	income
Fixed Income:	50%	high quality long-term
Foreign bonds:	10%	
Liquid assets:	10%	
Inflation hedges:	10%	

The next model is also on the aggressive side. It's recommended by mutual fund authority Sheldon Jacobs in his book *The Handbook for No-Load Fund Investors* (1993). His portfolios demonstrate how tricky the calculations can be.

The first portfolio he recommends is for younger people, and it consists of:

- long-term stock funds: 75%
- aggressive stock funds: 5%
- international stock funds: 20%

This portfolio would seem to be 100 percent invested in the stock market. But Jacobs has taken into consideration how much cash the particular funds in his portfolio contained at the time he recommended them: a weighted average of 12 percent. Besides, one fund, Fidelity Convertible, makes up 20 percent of the fund's assets, and that fund might be classified as a bond fund, not a stock fund—although Jacobs doesn't. Also, Jacobs' funds include some that buy bonds—Fidelity Equity-Income II and Vanguard/Windsor II. So the breakdown, very roughly, is

- 70% stocks
- 18% bonds
- 12% cash

Next is his preretirement portfolio, presumably for people in their fifties and early sixties. Here is Jacobs' suggested portfolio:

- long-term stocks: 55%
- international stocks: 20%
- bonds: 25%

The funds in this portfolio were a weighted average of 9 percent in cash, so the rough breakdown really is:

- stocks: 69% (long-term stocks: 51%; international stocks: 18%)
- bonds: 22%
- cash: 9%

The final portfolio is for retirees, and here's the breakdown:

- long-term stocks: 45%
- international stocks: 20%
- bonds: 35%

Here the funds are a weighted average of 8 percent in cash, and again a convertible-securities fund is classified as a stock fund. (If it weren't, the portfolio would be much heavier into bonds—even though one designated bond fund, T. Rowe Price Spectrum Income, holds some dividend-paying stocks.)

So a realistic breakdown would be:

- stocks: 52% (long-term stocks: 35%; international stocks: 17%)
- bonds: 40%
- cash: 8%

36

COMPARING TWO MODELS

Asset allocation guides weren't handed over to humankind on the summit of Mount Sinai. Even two models, published in the same magazine in the same year, contain key differences—even though both would be considered aggressive (people over age fifty are urged to have over 50 percent of their assets in the stock market).

Here is one asset allocation guide suggested by *Money* magazine (November 1993):

Ages 20 to 35

Large company stocks	25%
Small company stocks	25
International stocks	25
High-yield bonds	15
Convertible bonds	10

Stocks: 75%
Bonds: 25%

Ages 35 to 45

Large company stocks	20%
Small company stocks	10%
International stocks	20%
High-dividend stocks	20%
Corporate bonds	20%
International bonds	10%

Stocks: 70%
Bonds: 30%

Ages 45 to 55

Large company stocks	15% to 25%
International stocks	15% to 20%
High-dividend stocks	30%
Government securities	25%
International bonds	5% to 10%

Stocks: 65%
Bonds: 35%

Age 55 and over

    Large company stocks..15%
    International stocks 10%
    High-dividend stocks 35%
    International bond 10%
    Treasury securities 30%

Stocks: 60%
Bonds: 40%

Below is another asset allocation guide that appeared in *Money* magazine in a special summer issue the same year, a guide prepared with the help of the San Francisco investment advisers Bingham Osborn & Scarborough.

Single woman, 25, with $10,000
- stocks: 75% (large company 30%, small company 25%, foreign stock fund 20%)
- bonds: 25%

Differences from first model: This is identical with the other *Money* model, except that the large company stocks have shed 5%, foreign stock funds have gained 5%.

Married couple, mid-30s, $50,000
- stocks: 75% (30% large-company funds, 25% small-company funds, 20% foreign stock funds)
- domestic bond funds: 15%
- foreign bond funds: 5%
- money markets: 5%

Differences: the first model is only 70 percent in stocks, 30 percent in domestic and foreign bonds, and no money markets. The types of stock funds also vary: the percentage in small company stocks rose from 10 percent to 25 percent.

Married couple, early 50s, $250,000
- stocks: 60% (large-company 25%, small-company 20%, foreign stock funds 15%)
- domestic bonds: 30%
- foreign bonds: 5%
- money market: 5%

Differences: stocks lost 5 percent, small-company stocks

went from nothing to 20 percent, money markets gained 5 percent.

Married couple, early 60s, $350,000
- stocks: 40% (22% large-company stock funds, 11% small-company stock funds, 7% foreign stock funds)
- domestic bonds: 44%
- foreign bonds: 8%
- money market: 8%

Differences: stocks have dropped from 60 percent to 40 percent; bonds have climbed from 40 percent to 52 percent.

The point of this comparison, of course, is simply to demonstrate that asset allocation models are constructed by artists as well as by scientists.

37

ASSET ALLOCATION WITH FUNDS

The asset allocation model below specifies choices of mutual funds, so it is especially suitable for people who invest in 401(k) plans.

The options themselves include foreign, domestic growth, domestic growth and income, balanced, and income funds—five types of stock funds.

Fund Group	Conservative	Moderate	Aggressive
If your age is in the ...			
		20s and 30s	
Global growth	10%	20%	30%
Growth	—	25	45
Growth and income	40	35	15
Balanced	20	—	—
Income	30	20	10
Maximum in stocks	62%	80%	90%
		40s	
Global growth	10	20	30
Growth	—	—	30
Growth and income	30	25	20
Balanced	20	20	—
Income	40	35	20
Maximum in stocks	52%	57%	80%
		50s	
Global growth	5	10	15
Growth	—	—	20
Growth and income	20	25	25
Balanced	15	15	—
Income	60	50	40
Maximum in stocks	28%	38%	60%

	60s and older		
Global growth	5	10	15
Growth	—	—	15
Growth and income	10	20	20
Balanced	15	10	—
Income	70%	60	50
Maximum in stocks	18%	36%	50%

Paul Merriman, a mutual fund manager in Seattle, considers this model too conservative, pointing out that "under this scheme if you consider yourself conservative you are not allowed to have any, not any, of your money invested for growth once you reach the age of 40. For what is probably the majority of most people's lives, they [would be] shut off from participating in the long-term growth of equities in this country."

On the other hand, the model may be too aggressive in one respect: Nothing is allotted to money market funds.

38

REBALANCING

Let's say that you decide—because of your age, your risk level, and your prosperity—that you want to be 50 percent in stocks, 40 percent in fixed-income investments, and 10 percent in cash equivalents. You dollar-cost average your way into such a portfolio: invest in it gradually, perhaps over a year or two or three.

After your portfolio is set up, a few months elapse. The stock market has risen and the bond market has dipped. You are now 55 percent in stocks, 35 percent in fixed-income investments, and 10 percent in cash.

Obviously, your asset allocation is now riskier than you had originally intended.

Should you ride your winners and stick with your current asset allocation? (This would be the "buy and hold forever" strategy.)

Should you retreat to the starting line—sell enough of your stocks so you're back to 50 percent, and add whatever you've sold to your fixed-income investments, bringing that percentage up to 40 percent?

Should you put more money on your winners—invest more into stocks, less into bonds? Isn't it true that "the trend is your friend"?

Or, instead of waiting for a significant imbalance in your portfolio, should you automatically rebalance at regular intervals—every three months, every six months, every year?

No one knows the right answers, but the most sensible thing to do seems to be to rebalance whenever your portfolio gets badly out of whack. That way, you lock in your gains by selling whatever has gone up dramatically... and you buy securities that seem cheap.

A study by Stine and Lewis of Stephen F. Austin University published in the April 1992 issue of the *Journal of*

Financial Planning concluded that rebalancing when a portfolio is a good distance away from its original is best.

The researchers had studied how various kinds of rebalancing techniques fared over three years, five years, ten years, fifteen years, and twenty years. The most profitable, they found, was rebalancing when there was a 7.5 percent to 10 percent misalignment.

"The passive portfolio," they wrote, "must be rebalanced to maintain a level of risk exposure consistent with the investor's objectives.... In most cases, the investor would be advised to rebalance only when the portfolio reaches a predetermined level of risk exposure rather than to make the adjustments on a calendar basis. This has the advantage of producing a narrower range of possible stock weights and, in most cases, requires fewer rebalances....

"A reasonable strategy is to rebalance whenever the stock weights vary 7.5 percent to 10 percent from their original position. Over all the investment horizons, this strategy does better than annual rebalancing.... However, if the portfolio manager elects to follow a calendar strategy, rebalancing quarterly or semiannually is too frequent and the annual rebalancing strategy appears to produce the best result."

The Capital Consulting Group recommends rebalancing a conservative portfolio every year; a moderate portfolio, every six months; and an aggressive portfolio, every three months. The thinking seems to be that aggressive portfolios get bent out of shape faster than conservative ones. While that is probably true, a case can be made that the more conservative you are, the more frequently you should rebalance—to keep your portfolio more stable.

You will also be changing your asset allocation model as you grow older. You'll need your money sooner; you cannot wait so long for markets to bounce back.

When should you switch to a more conservative portfolio? You could set target days: your sixtieth birthday, for instance. But making such drastic shifts in your asset-allocation model all at once seems hazardous.

It would probably be more sensible to change your asset

allocation more gradually. On your fifty-fifth birthday, perhaps, or your sixtieth, you might begin moving more into bonds and cash equivalents, for instance. And you could take advantage of high stock markets to sell stocks, and high interest rates to buy bonds.

To rebalance your portfolio, you can change your entire allocation by increments of 25 percent. Some plans will enable you to proceed more slowly—by changing the allocation of only your new contributions.

39

DOLLAR-COST AVERAGING

If you regularly salt away part of your salary into a 401(k) plan, you are in effect practicing dollar-cost averaging. This is the case whether you are paid weekly, biweekly, or monthly.

Dollar-cost averaging (DCA) means investing the same amount of money—regularly. (Examples: $100 every other week, $1,000 every three months.) DCA works best with the stock market, because stocks as a group tend to bob up and down but wind up higher in the long run.

One benefit of DCA is that you won't buy a lot of shares of a stock, or a group of stocks, just when prices are unusually high.

There's another benefit.

Let's say that a stock is $50 a share in January, $100 in March, $25 in May, $20 in July. You're encouraged in March, and buy $5,000 worth of shares. You wind up with 50 shares. (Commissions and other costs are being ignored.) In May, your shares are worth $1,250 and you are worried sick. But you clench your teeth and hang on. "I'm a long-term investor," you tell yourself. By July, with the price down to $20 a share and with your having lost 80 percent of your investment, you decide to cut bait—and sell just so as to keep a measly $1,000 of your money.

Question: What happened to the shares of that stock in September?

Answer: That's unpredictable. The price may have dropped some more—or gone up—or remained the same.

But let's say that you decided to buy $1,250 worth shares every other month instead of springing for the whole $5,000 all at once. You buy 25 shares in January, 12.5 in March, 50 in May, and 62.5 in July. In July you would have wound up

114

with 150 shares, worth $20 each. You still have a loss, but it's only $2,000, not $4,000. And when you decide to hold onto the stock, or sell, or buy more shares, you'll probably be in a more composed frame of mind.

There's a third benefit of DCA: Even if a stock or mutual fund falls, you may make money. Reason: when you practice DCA, you buy the most shares when the prices are low.

Let's say that you buy $200 worth of shares of a no-sales-charge mutual fund every month.

Price Per Share	Month	Shares
$10	February	20
$ 5	March	40
$ 4	April	50
$ 6	May	33.33
$ 7	June	28.57
$ 3	July	66.66
$ 9	August	22.22

At this point, you decide to sell. Will you have a large capital loss—or, thanks to dollar-cost averaging, a small loss?

You started buying at $10 and sold at $9. But you bought the most shares when prices were very low, and bought the fewest shares when prices were high.

You spent $1,400—$200 for seven months.

The final price per share was $9.

You own 260.78 shares. At $9 a share, they're worth $2,347.02.

You have a capital gain of about $947.

Dollar-cost averaging has drawbacks. If a stock or a fund goes up, you would have been better off plunking down your money all at once.

If a stock or fund goes down and stays down, you would have been better off not investing in the first place and not dollar-cost averaging afterwards.

But the worst flaw of DCA may be that it's hard to get people to practice it. In February (in the example above), when the price is high ($10), they invest all their money: $1,400. In July, when the price is very low, they despair and sell out. Instead of making $947, they lose $980.

115

Recently, various academic studies have indicated that, most of the time, you are better off investing a lump sum directly in the market instead of dollar-cost averaging.

The trouble with these studies is that (a) they didn't consider the degree of loss you may have suffered when you invested at a bad time, and how long it would have taken your investment to heal, and (b) they didn't consider the danger that you might panic and sell after sustaining a major loss.

Let's say that you have all of your 401(k) money in guaranteed investment contracts. But you have now decided to move into the stock market. How long should it take you to dollar-cost average a large sum of cash or fixed-income investments into stocks?

John Markese of the American Association of Individual Investors in Chicago has said two or three years.

But if you are investing in a market-timing fund, like Fidelity Asset Manager or Vanguard Asset Allocation, you can certainly move faster. If you invest in a balanced fund (which has stocks and bonds) or a fund that tries to buy undervalued stocks, you can probably also move a little faster. There's less danger.

If you are withdrawing money from a 401(k) plan and putting it into another retirement vehicle, you can maintain the same asset allocation with your new portfolio. If your 401(k) plan was 50 percent in stocks and 50 percent in bonds, you can immediately invest the same way with a rollover IRA. You might want to use the opportunity, though, to modify your asset allocation in line with your age.

40

MODEST MARKET-TIMING

One of the worst mistakes that investors can make is trying to time the market—trying to avoid bear markets and enjoy bull markets.

Most investors should simply follow their asset-allocation models, come heck or high water. They should not make sudden, drastic changes in their portfolios—for example, selling their stocks when stocks nosedive, moving into stocks as stocks begin to climb. There is even a term for what may happen to investors who desert one area that is doing poorly and flee to another—that suddenly begins performing just as poorly. Getting "whipsawed."

Investors should avoid aggressive, unrestrained market-timing.

But they might consider milk-and-water market-timing.

If you are convinced that the stock market is overpriced, or that the economy is going into a downturn, you need not bet the ranch. You can make small bets.

Let's say that the newspapers, magazines, or newsletters you rely on and people whose opinion you trust persuade you that the stock market is too high and you should take cover. Let's say that your portfolio is 60 percent in stocks, 10 percent in cash, and 30 percent in fixed-income investments. Here's what you can do:

- Diversify your stock investments more. For example, if you can invest in shares of a foreign stock fund but you own little or none, move a percentage of your U.S. stock fund into the foreign stock fund.
- Move your stock investments to more conservative stocks. Go from a growth fund to a growth-and-income fund or to an equity-income fund. You could move modestly: increasing your equity-income fund by 10 percent, shrinking your growth fund by 10 percent.

- Move more into cash. Shift your asset-allocation model from 60 percent in stocks and 10 percent in cash to 55 percent in stocks to 15 percent in cash.
- Move more into fixed-income investments. You could shift from a pure stock fund to a balanced fund, which has up to 40 percent in bonds.
- Practice passive market-timing. Just rebalance your portfolio whenever it's badly unbalanced (see Key 38) and invest regularly—so as to practice dollar-cost averaging (see Key 39).

If you practice these modest forms of market-timing, you may develop the courage you need to invest more aggressively in the stock market in general.

You might also consider such modest market-timing steps with regard to fixed-income investments if you think that interest rates are going up. You could invest more in foreign bonds, shorten your maturities, or put more into money-market funds.

41

CASHING IN YOUR 401(K)

Once you reach age fifty-nine and a half, you are entitled to withdraw the money in your 401(k) plan permanently, and without penalty.

If you are under fifty-nine and a half, you may be allowed to withdraw money from your 401(k) plan, and not pay it back, only for reasons of "hardship":

- to buy your first residence (not a summer home)
- to pay for college tuition
- to avoid eviction or mortgage foreclosure

You must prove that you have no other source of money. You must pay taxes on the money withdrawn, along with a 10 percent penalty. And some plans require that you not be able to make a new contribution for a year.

For more about hardship withdrawals, see Key 43. To borrow from your 401(k), see Key 42.

Someone can also permanently withdraw money for these reasons:

- death
- disability
- retirement
- termination of employment.

Avoiding the 20 Percent Trap

Let's say that you're retiring or leaving your employer, and getting a lump-sum distribution from your 401(k) plan. (A "lump-sum distribution" is just a big pile of your money.) And because you're under fifty-nine and a half, you would have to pay a 10 percent tax penalty on whatever you withdraw (along with current income taxes) if you don't roll over the money into an individual retirement account within 60 days.

So, not being immediately needful of cash, you roll over the money within those 60 days.

Unfortunately, that would be a mistake. Your employer

would be obligated to keep 20 percent of your money—to give to the IRS.

You would get that 20 percent back later, when you proved that you did roll over the money. But in the meantime 20 percent of your lump-sum distribution wouldn't be earning a thing for you. It would be earning money for Uncle Sam.

There's something you can do: roll over another 20 percent of the distribution, using money out of your own pocket. In other words, you would receive a big sum of money—and have to roll over 120 percent of that.

Here's an example:

Let's say that on January 1 you have $100,000 in your 401(k), and you ask your employer for all the money. Your employer would withhold $20,000 and send you a check for $80,000. Now, to shelter your entire $100,000 payout, you would need an extra $20,000. If you don't happen to have $20,000 lying around, only $80,000 will be treated as a rollover, and the $20,000 remainder would be subject to taxes—and possibly to an early-withdrawal penalty if you don't kick in that extra $20,000.

If you do owe taxes on the distribution (because you didn't roll over all the money), Uncle Sam will use that 20 percent to pay the taxes you'll owe. You will also owe a 10 percent tax penalty for taking out the money before you reached fifty-nine and a half.

Fortunately, you can withdraw the money before you're fifty-nine and a half without penalty and without your employer's withholding 20 percent if you're disabled—or if you withdraw the money not as a lump sum but in regular payments according to your estimated lifespan (in other words, as an annuity).

You can also avoid the 20 percent withholding altogether if you play your cards right.

You can arrange for a financial institution to handle the rollover for you, via a "transfer," where the money is never actually in your hot little hands.

Ask a financial institution (like a mutual fund) to give you an IRA transfer form, fill it out, and obtain an account number—even though there's no money in your rollover IRA yet. Then present the form to your employer to transfer the distribution.

This option lets your retirement assets continue to grow tax-deferred. But don't mix up your distribution with an IRA you already have. Set up a new, "conduit" IRA. And don't ever add anything to this conduit IRA.

The National Center for Financial Education suggests that you have your distribution transferred into a government securities money market fund—the safest possible investment—while you ponder how to spread out the money into a well-diversified portfolio. You might have a good mutual fund company prepare the paperwork to accept your distribution into one of its government securities money market funds—although any mutual fund's money market fund or bank's money market deposit account would do almost as well.

Next, write a letter like this to your employer:

Rollover Letter to Your Employer . . .

Re: Lump-sum distribution from my retirement plan

[*Date*]

Dear sirs:

Please accept this letter as my specific instruction for you to provide the proper forms to me so that I may request a lump-sum distribution from my pension plan. I wish to direct my distribution funds into a rollover IRA account with [*fill in name of financial institution*] government securities money market fund [or other money market fund or deposit account].

Enclosed are the completed forms from the fund sponsors, so that they will be able to accept the check directly from you into a rollover IRA account.

The reason for this request is to keep you from having to send 20 percent of my distribution to the IRS, and so that 100 percent of my funds may be rolled over into the above-named account.

Please let me know if there is anything else you need to

make this transaction occur smoothly. You can telephone me at [*fill in office number*] or at [*fill in home number*].

[*Employee signature*] _____
[*Address*]

[*Spouse signature*] _____
[*Address*]

Source: National Center for Financial Education, P.O. Box 34070, San Diego, CA 92163.

You have still other ways to deal with the possibility of your employer's sending the IRS 20 percent of your distribution:

- Reduce the withholding on your wages from the beginning of the year, while you are still working. That would partly offset the 20 percent withholding on your distribution.
- Reduce any estimated-tax payments you would normally make.
- Defer the distribution until the end of the tax year, and promptly file your tax return at the beginning of the next year. That way, you would get back your 20 percent as soon as possible.
- Leave your savings in your employer's plan. If your assets in the plan exceed $3,500, your former employer is required to let you keep the money there.
- Transfer your distribution into your new employer's plan. Some employers may insist on a one-year waiting period, in which case you might set up a conduit IRA (step 2).

42

BORROWING FROM YOUR 401(K)

The cheapest place to get a loan is from generous relatives. The second cheapest is a loan that uses your home as collateral—assuming that you own a home. A good portion of the interest will be tax-deductible (if you itemize). A third good source is your 401(k) plan, assuming that you really need the money.

Most 401(k)s let you borrow money, whereas most defined-benefit plans don't.

Perhaps 25 percent of all 401(k) participants borrow from their plans. That doesn't mean that you should—unless you know what you're doing, and you have a good reason.

The most common reasons people give for borrowing 401(k) money:

- to pay off other debts;
- to pay college tuition;
- for emergencies.

When you borrow from a 401(k) plan, you're really borrowing your own money. That's why you can get the money without a credit check and without red tape in general. And that's why the interest rate that you pay will be reasonable compared with general rates. (No, you cannot deduct the interest.)

Payments will probably be deducted from your paycheck.

You cannot borrow all of your 401(k) money. You can borrow up to 50 percent of your balance that's "vested" (what you're entitled to if you leave your job). In any case, you cannot borrow more than $50,000.

The loans must be repaid within five years—unless you use the money to buy your main home. In that case, you can have from ten to thirty years to repay the loan, the time depending on the particular plan. By the way, while mortgage interest is usually tax-deductible, it's not if you borrow money to pay that interest.

Where does the interest go? To your own 401(k)—which means that you're breaking even (though your money isn't earning anything while it's out on loan). It's in effect a no-interest loan—not surprising, because you're both borrower and lender.

But you'll be losing the possible appreciation on the 401(k) money you withdraw. If the money had remained there, it might have made you a handsome amount of money.

What if you take the money and use it as a downpayment on a house? In that case, the appreciation you may have lost by taking out the money will be offset—in two ways. First, you will have less money to borrow for a mortgage (so you save paying interest on the money you didn't borrow). Also, with a larger downpayment, you can perhaps knock down the interest rate on the entire mortgage.

So, is it a good idea to borrow from your 401(k) plan? It depends on how your 401(k) investments perform—and what you use the borrowed money for. If your 401(k) plan is all in low-paying money market funds, and you use the money to buy a car you need, for cash instead of borrowing the money, you may be ahead of the game.

But if the 401(k) money is in the stock market and you miss a swift, sharp rally, and you use the borrowed money to frolic off on a vacation, you will have in effect lost a bundle.

That's why, in general, it's best to borrow from the part of your 401(k) plan that's paying the least: a money market fund or a guaranteed investment contract.

What if you leave your job while you owe money on the loan? If you don't repay it immediately, it will be treated as a distribution. You'll probably have to pay income taxes on the money and—if you're under fifty-nine and a half and not disabled—you'll also owe a 10 percent tax penalty for having taken an early distribution.

43

IN CASE OF HARDSHIP

A hardship distribution from a 401(k) plan can be made by someone with immediate and heavy financial needs. According to the rules, these needs must not be able to be met reasonably from other financial resources the person may have.

The plan must set up uniform and nondiscriminatory standards for hardship withdrawals. That is, the rules must apply to everyone—and not favor any one group, such as the wealthy.

The amount withdrawn cannot exceed the amount required to meet a person's immediate needs.

Some plans specify that only contributions that the employee has made can be withdrawn—not the earnings on those contributions, and no employer matching contributions can be withdrawn for reasons of hardship. Excess contributions—those that weren't tax-deductible—also cannot be withdrawn for hardship reasons.

Even with a hardship withdrawal, if the person taking out the money is under fifty-nine and a half there will be a 10 percent tax penalty. And the money withdrawn must be included as ordinary income on the person's tax return.

A particular plan will describe what qualifies as a financial need.

44

GETTING HELP

If you have questions about your 401(k) plan—the rules, how to invest, how to withdraw your money—the first place to go is to your employer's human resources or personnel department.

Your employer may give you literature to read. Or refer you to the investment adviser who manages the money, and agents for the adviser may answer your questions.

Other literature can also help. You might want to subscribe to various newsletters that report on mutual funds, or obtain the publications of mutual funds themselves, or of mutual fund organizations. (See Key 22.)

A good source of information is The 401(k) Association, One Summit Square, Doublewoods Road and Route 413, Langhorne, PA 19047. The group, headed by Ted Benna, publishes a newsletter and financial software. Dues for the first year are on two levels: $95, which includes software, and $35 without software. After the first year, the fee is $35. Phone: 215-579-8830.

Ted Benna is the man who in 1980 noticed the provision in the 1978 tax law that led to the mushrooming of 401(k) retirement plans.

Among Benna's goals is to make 401(k) plans better—for example, by persuading employers to provide more options: "As plans mature and become larger," he says, "employers should probably be providing eight to 12 fund options, not three or four."

For tax advice, look for a certified public accountant, or at least an enrolled agent. A 401(k) plan may involve lots of money, and you may make costly errors unless you seek outside tax help.

For investment advice, consider a certified financial planner. Planners are usually better choices than accountants (unless the accountants have special training), stockbrokers, banking officials, and insurance agents.

For the names of CPAs who have financial-planning training, contact the American Institute of Certified Public Accountants, Personal Financial Planning Divsion, 1211 Avenue of the Americas, New York, NY 10036.

Some of the best financial planners are members of the Registry of Financial Planning Practitioners. Write to the International Institute for Financial Planning, 2 Concourse Parkway, Atlanta, GA 30328.

For Certified Financial Planners in general, write to the Institute of Certified Financial Planners, 10065 East Harvard Avenue, Denver, CO 80231.

For fee-only planners, write to the National Association of Fee-Only Personal Financial Advisors, 1130 Lake Cook Road, Suite 105, Buffalo Grove, IL 60089.

Check whether the particular planner you are considering specializes in clients with money in retirement plans. Find out how long he or she has been in business (four years is a rough minimum). Interview a planner's references, a key question being: would you hire him or her again? Make sure that the planner's fee is reasonable. Be skeptical if the planner wants you to pay for continuing guidance.

In general, you shouldn't have to pay a lot of money for help in managing your retirement money. This book in itself should tell you virtually all you need to know.

45

THE HISTORY OF 401(K) PLANS

The first pensions for industrial companies began in Prussia in the 1860s, when workers started receiving benefits when they retired at sixty-five. (Bismarck is supposed to have chosen that age.) The idea quickly spread to the United States.

In 1875, American Express Co.—not the financial services company of today but a freight service—became the first U.S. company to set up an employer-sponsored plan. Next was the Baltimore and Ohio Railroad, in 1880. Public utilities and banks soon followed suit.

Pensions became commonplace early in the twentieth century.

In 1926, the Revenue Act exempted from income taxes any employer contributions to pensions. In 1929, employer-sponsored pensions covered about 15 percent of private-sector workers.

With the Great Depression, many companies ended their pension contributions or scotched their plans altogether. Almost all union plans also terminated in the early 1930s. By 1938, there were only about 500 plans, which was 100 more than before the stock market crash of 1929.

In 1935, Congress passed the Social Security and Railroad Retirement Systems Act. By 1946, the number of pension plans had reached about 7,000, covering three million employees.

In 1962, Congress allowed the self-employed to set up tax-deferred retirement plans, called HR-10s or Keogh Plans.

In 1974, Congress passed the Employee Retirement Income Security Act (ERISA), which created individual retirement accounts along with the Pension Benefit Guaranty

Corporation to insure the promised benefits of defined-benefit plans against the plans' being terminated.

In 1986, higher-income workers could no longer deduct contributions to IRAs.

The 401(k) plan was named after the section of the Internal Revenue Service code that authorized them, part of the Retirement Act of 1978. It was not until November 1981, though, that the IRS made it clear that employees could put pretax dollars of their own into the plans. In 1982, just 2 percent of the Fortune 100 companies offered 401(k) plans.

Effective on January 1, 1994, employers could obtain some protection against lawsuits from employees for 401(k) investments that performed poorly if they follow certain guidelines. To obtain this limited liability, an employer's 401(k) plan must

- offer at least three investment alternatives, not including the employer's stock in the employer's company, with different levels of risk and possible return. A guaranteed investment contract may or may not qualify as one of the three choices, depending on the circumstances.
- allow employees to make transfers between their choices at least once every four months.
- provide information regarding the objectives of each investment alternative, such as prospectuses and information about commissions.

QUESTIONS AND ANSWERS

Should everyone without exception invest in a 401(k) plan?

If your contributions are matched to any extent whatsoever, you should without question invest in your employer's plan. Otherwise, you are saying "No, thank you" to free money.

If your contributions are not matched by your employer, you might skip investing in a 401(k) plan if (a) you can defer a good deal of other income from taxation (via a Keogh plan, for instance, if you have self-employment income) and (b) if you are dubious of your company's plan because it doesn't offer enough choices or because your company's investment record is poor. (Even if the investment record is poor, though, you can always choose a conservative investment, like a money market fund or a guaranteed investment contract.)

If you feel that you can't spare any money at all, see if you can lower the tax withholdings from your salary check by increasing the number of exemptions you claim on Form W-4. After all, by contributing to a 401(k) plan, you will be lowering your tax liability.

What do you mean by "matching"?

Let's say that you earn $20,000 a year, and you want to contribute 10 percent of your salary to a 401(k) plan. That means $2,000 annually. Your employer might match up to 3 percent of your salary, dollar for dollar. That means your employer would give you 3 percent of $20,000, or $600. So, if you contribute at least $600, or 3 percent of your salary, you will at least double your money.

What percentage should I contribute?

It depends on what you can afford, and what you want to save money for. If you're saving to start a business in a few years, or for a child's college education, or to buy a house, you probably shouldn't tie up much of your money in a retirement plan. While you can withdraw money from a plan in cases of hardship, you will have a 10 percent tax penalty to pay. Still, if you're saving for your retirement, be generous. People are usually urged to save 10 percent of their incomes. You might start with saving 5 percent, then bring up the percentage later on.

What's the most I can contribute?

Plans have their own maximums, but usually it's about 13 percent of your salary. In 1994, the highest amount of pretax money that you could put away was $9,240—not including your employer's contributions. Including those contributions, the maximum was the lesser of $30,000 or 25 percent of your salary.

What should I invest in?

If you don't know much about investing, start conservatively—with a money market fund or a guaranteed investment contract (GIC). A GIC is like a certificate of deposit offered by a bank, but it isn't insured by the federal government. In the meantime, read up about investments.

My 401(k) plan offers me a stock fund, a GIC, a balanced fund, and a money market fund. I can invest 25 percent of my regular contributions in each of them. What should I do? What's a balanced fund?

Decide what your asset allocation should be—how much you want in stocks, in bonds, and in cash or cash equivalents. The answer will depend upon your age (the younger you are, the more you can tilt toward stocks); your prosperity (the richer you are, the more risk you can take); your risk tolerance (which is roughly equal to your sophistication—how unlikely you are to panic and sell when the market goes into a swoon).

Let's say you're thirty, you want to save for your retirement, and you've vowed not to sell in a panic if the stock market goes down and stays down. You might have 75 percent in stocks, 25 percent in fixed-income investments (like GICs).

A balanced fund is a good, solid choice for most investors. Typically it's 60 percent in stocks, 40 percent in bonds. So you will enjoy a healthy exposure to the stock market, but have bonds for income and for stability.

What if I need the money after I've contributed it. Am I out of luck?

Most 401(k) plans let you withdraw money permanently, for hardship, or borrow money. Check your company's rules.

Could I lose money in a 401(k) plan? Could my employer keep my contributions?

Yes . . . and no. Certainly you can lose money. If you buy shares of a stock fund, and the stock market plunges, you will have a loss. If you buy shares of a bond fund and interest rates rise, you may also have a loss. On the other hand, you can't lose money in a money market fund and it's very unlikely you'll lose money in a GIC. But you won't make much money, either, in such conservative investments.

No, your employer cannot keep your contributions. It's your money, now and forever.

How can I tell if the company managing my money has done a good job?

Your employer should give you a report on the manager's track record—comparing the manager's performance with some index, like the Standard & Poor's 500 Stock Index. Another good way to evaluate a fund is to compare its performance with the performances of similar funds—a balanced fund against other balanced funds, for example.

If the manager also runs a similar public fund, you can check how the public fund has performed by examining issues of *Morningstar Mutual Funds* or *Value Line Mutual Funds* in a library.

My 401(k) plan offers a foreign stock fund. How much should I invest in that fund?

First decide how much you want to have in the stock market. (The rule is that no one is brave enough to have over 80 percent in stocks.) Next, you might follow a rough rule: Don't have more than 30 percent of your stock portfolio in foreign stocks.

When should I change my allocations?

In general, don't try to time the market on your own. Even the most sophisticated investors sometimes get blown out of the water when they try.

Amateurs buy stocks after they have gone up for a while—and are overpriced. Amateurs sell stocks after they have gone down for a while—and are underpriced. Amateurs who determine to hang on through thick and thin are rapidly ascending to the level of sophisticated investors.

If you're determined to market-time, follow the advice in a reputable newsletter, like Standard & Poor's *The Outlook*: the front page of each issue suggests the percentages you might have in stocks, bonds, and cash.

Consider changing your allocation if it now differs drastically from what you originally decided on. This "rebalancing" might take place whenever you are 10 percentage points away from your originally allocation model. For example, if you set out to be 50 percent in stocks and 50 percent in guaranteed investment contracts, and you're now 70 percent in stocks, 30 percent in GICs, you might sell your stocks, investing the proceeds into GICs, until you're fifty-fifty again.

What if your financial situation changes—because you've inherited a lot of money, won the lottery, or landed a new job (and doubled your salary)? You can become a more aggressive investor.

As you grow older, though, become a more conservative investor. Gradually lower your exposure to stocks and beef up your exposure to fixed-income investments.

GLOSSARY

Aggressive growth fund fund that seeks maximum capital gains. It usually remains fully invested in stocks at all times; it buys small, speculative companies and depressed stocks; and it may employ techniques like selling short and using leverage. Aggressive growth funds tend to be especially volatile.

All-weather fund fund that does well in bull and bear markets.

Appreciation growth in value of an asset.

Asset allocation fund fund that either keeps a fixed percentage of its assets in various instruments—bonds, stocks, precious-metals stocks, real-estate stocks—or varies the percentages, depending on where the fund managers think the investment markets are heading. A true asset allocation fund has some investments in inflation-resistant hard assets (precious metals, real estate).

Balanced fund fund that invests in both stocks and bonds—typically 60 percent in stocks, 40 percent in bonds.

Barbell way of investing in fixed-income securities, so that short maturities are balanced by longer-term maturities.

Basic value investing investment strategy that concentrates on buying seemingly undervalued stocks, based on their price-earnings ratios, price to book value, and other indicators.

Basis point in bond yields, 0.01%. If a bond's yield goes from 10% to 11%, it has increased by 100 basis points.

Bear market time when stocks (or other investments) keep sinking in value, despite occasional rallies, or when stocks remain at depressed levels.

Blue chip stock of a large, prosperous, well-established company. The 30 stocks in the Dow Jones Industrial Average—including IBM, AT&T, Exxon—are unquestionably blue chips.

Bond debt instrument that pays a regular interest, whether or not the company issuing the bond is making money. Debt instruments are "senior" securities: their holders must be paid before a company pays owners of its stock.

Bond fund fund that invests mainly in corporate, municipal, or U.S. Treasury securities. Such a fund emphasizes income rather than capital gains.

Bond rating system of grading bonds on their ability to pay their obligations. Standard & Poor's ratings range from "AAA" (extremely unlikely to default) to "D" (in default). Moody's ratings are similar.

Bottom up method of investing in which the investor concentrates on buying attractive stocks, whatever the broad trends of the market or the economy. *See* **Top down**.

Broker/dealer firm, like Merrill Lynch, that buys and sells load mutual funds and other securities to the public.

Bull market time when stocks (or other securities) keep climbing in value, despite occasional stumbles. Sometimes the boundary between bull and bear markets isn't sharp.

Bullet way of investing in fixed-income securities in which the maturities are neither short term nor long term but intermediate term.

Buy and hold investment strategy that entails buying shares of stock or a mutual fund for the long term and selling them only in special circumstances, such as after a long-term loss. *See* **Market timing**.

Cash equivalents short-term obligations, like Treasury bills.

Certificates of deposit conservative debt instruments provided by a bank or savings and loan, with maturities varying from months to several years. Usually there are penalties if an investor cashes in a CD before maturity. With a floating rate CD, the interest rate changes in line with the prime rate.

Common stock security representing ownership of a public corporation's assets.

Contribution money you put into a retirement plan.

Corporate bond fund fund that invests in corporate bonds, which may be high rated or low rated, and have short-term, medium-term, or long-term maturities.

Current yield dividends paid to investors, expressed as a percentage of the current price.

Defined benefit plan retirement plan in which an employer is responsible for investing employees' money. *See* **Defined contribution plan**.

Defined contribution plan retirement plan, like a 401(k), that allows employees to invest pre-tax money for their retirement. Their contributions are limited ("defined"). Employees manage their own investments. *See* **Defined benefit plan**.

Distributions payments that a mutual fund makes to its shareholders, from the sales of its securities, from interest, from dividends—or a return of the shareholder's original investment.

Diversification spreading investments over a variety of different securities, to reduce risk.

Dividends money (or stock) that a company pays the owners of its stock, usually four times a year.

Dollar-cost averaging investing the same amount of money at regular intervals, so that when securities are low-priced you buy more shares. A method of diversifying the prices at which you buy securities.

Dow Jones Industrial Average model for the stock market as a whole. It consists of 30 blue-chip stocks.

Equities stocks, real estate, other assets that an investor owns, as opposed to bonds, where an investor lends money.

Equity-income type of mutual fund that concentrates on high-paying common stocks.

Event risk the danger that a bond will lose value because of special situations, such as the issuer being subjected to a leveraged buyout and acquiring a great deal of new debt.

Fair-weather fund fund that excels in bull markets but gives a mediocre or poor performance in bear markets. *See* **Foul-weather fund**.

Family group of mutual funds under one umbrella, typically consisting of at least a stock fund, a bond fund, and a money market fund.

Fixed-income fund fund that invests mainly in bonds and preferred stock.

Flexible *See* **asset allocation**.

Formula investing investing according to mechanical techniques, such as dollar-cost averaging.

Foul-weather fund fund that excels in bear markets, one explanation being that the fund invests in securities that are already undervalued. *See* **Fair-weather fund**.

401(k) plan retirement plan set up by an employer that allows employees to set aside a certain percentage of their salaries, before taxes, for retirement. Often the employer matches the employees' contributions up to a point.

403(b) plan retirement plan for employees of public institutions, like schools.

General obligation bonds bonds that pay holders from their basic taxing authority—as opposed to revenue bonds.

Global fund one that invests in foreign as well as domestic stocks.

GNMA fund fund that invests in mortgage securities issued by the Government National Mortgage Association.

Government bond fund fund that invests mostly in Treasuries, but also possibly in government agency bonds and mortgage-backed securities.

Growth and income fund fund that invests in growth stocks as well as high-income, blue chip stocks.

Growth fund fund that invests in companies that seem to have bright futures in view of their growth rates.

Guaranteed investment contract investment, like a certificate of deposit, offered by an insurance company for 401(k) investors.

Hedge fund fund that not only invests in securities but may also sell short or write options, in order to protect itself from losses.

Income fund fund that stresses current income rather than growth of capital. Such funds may be invested in high-yielding stocks and in bonds, but mainly in bonds.

Index model of an investment market—stocks, bonds, utilities, health-care stocks, and so forth.

Index fund fund that attempts to emulate the performance of an index, like the Standard & Poor's 500 or the Shearson-Lehman Bond Index.

Individual retirement account (IRA) retirement plan that enables relatively low-income employees, or those with no pension coverage, to save up to $2,000 a year tax-free.

Interest regular payments from a borrower to a lender in return for the loan.

International fund fund that invests in the securities of foreign corporations or governments.

Investment grade bonds bonds rated "BBB," Standard & Poor's fourth-highest category, and above.

Investment objectives goals of a mutual fund, such as long-term capital gains, with income secondary.

Junk bonds bonds rated "BB" or below by Standard & Poor's. Such bonds are not so safe as investment grade bonds, but they pay higher interest. Also called "high yield bonds."

Ladder arranging the maturities of one's fixed-income investments so they become due at different times—such as one year, two years, and three years.

Liquidity measure of how readily an asset can be sold for cash. If an asset can readily be sold, but at a loss, its liquidity is compromised. In this respect, a money market fund is far more liquid than a stock fund.

Market-timing attempting to buy securities near the end of a bear market and to sell them near the end of a bull market—in other words, to buy low and sell high. *See* **Buy and hold**.

Maturity when a loan—or a bond—is due to be paid off by the debtor or by the issuing company.

Money-market fund fund that invests in debt obligations with average maturities of no more than 90 days. To keep the principal unchanging, usually at $1 a share, the fund varies the yield. Banks' funds are called money market deposit accounts.

Mortgage-backed securities shares of a pool of mortgages, issued by Fannie Mae (Federal National Mortgage Association), Freddie Mac (Federal Home Loan Mortgage Corporation), or Ginnie Mae (Government National Mortgage Association). Investors receive regular payments of principal and interest from the underlying mortgages.

Net asset value price per share of a fund: the fund's net assets divided by the number of shares outstanding.

Net assets value of a fund's holdings, minus debts, such as taxes owed.

No-load fund that does not charge a front-end commission. A "pure" no-load also has no deferred sales charge, and typically no redemption fee and no 12b-1 fee.

Open-end investment company fund that can continually issue more shares and thus add to its net assets. Such a fund also buys shares directly from its customers and sells shares directly to its customers. *See* **Closed-end investment company**.

Over-the-counter market in which securities are bought and sold through dealers, not on the floor of an exchange. OTC stocks are typically those of smaller companies.

Performance how well a fund has fared over a certain period of time, usually measured by capital gains, dividends, and interest the fund has earned.

Portfolio various securities held by an individual or a fund.

Portfolio manager person or committee that makes buy-and-sell decisions for a fund.

Premium percentage by which a security's price exceeds its net asset value per share. A bond paying high interest may trade at a premium.

Price-earnings ratio price per share of a stock, divided by its last 12 months of earnings (or estimated earnings for the next year). The P/E ratio indicates a stock's popularity by reflecting how much investors are willing to pay for its earning power.

Prospectus official document describing a mutual fund. It must be furnished to investors.

Qualified retirement plan with contributions that are tax-deferred.

Rebalancing changing one's assets allocation back to the original model after it has deviated. If the model allocation was 50 percent stocks, 40 percent bonds, and 10 percent cash, the portfolio might be rebalanced if the percentages changed over time.

Redemption fee charge a fund may levy, especially if an investor sells shares purchased recently.

Revenue bonds bonds that pay their holders from money the issuer earns—as from a turnpike authority—rather than from taxes.

Risk either the volatility of an instrument, or the possibility that the investment will lose value.

Risk tolerance ability of a person to accept what may be temporary losses from an investment.

Sales charge commission an investor must pay to buy shares of certain load mutual funds or of a limited partnership.

Sector stocks in one industry.

Secular long-term.

Securities stocks, bonds, options, warrants, or other instruments that signify a corporation's obligations to an investor.

Securities and Exchange Commission (SEC) federal agency, created in 1934, that administers the securities laws.

Small company fund fund of small-company stocks—the size usually being measured in terms of capitalization, which is stock price times shares outstanding.

Specialty fund that restricts its horizon to certain stocks: health care, regional banks, utilities, gold, and so forth.

Spread difference between the bid and the offer prices on a stock or bond.

Standard & Poor's 500 popular microcosm of the stock market, based on the prices of 500 widely held common stocks.

Standard deviation volatility of an investment, measured by comparing its average price with the degree of its ups and downs.

Stock *see* **Common stock**.

Time horizon how long you can remain invested before you will need your principal. The longer your time horizon, the greater the chance that you will escape needing your money in a down market

Top down method of investing in which the investor looks at general economic trends, then decides which industries and companies will benefit. *See* **Bottom up**.

Total return profit or loss that a mutual fund has achieved over a period of time, including capital gains or losses, interest and dividends, and expenses. It is expressed as a percentage of the original value of the assets.

Treasury debts of the U.S. government. The maturities of Treasury bills are up to one year, of notes, two to ten years, and of bonds, ten to thirty years.

Turnover ratio trading activity of a mutual fund, calculated by dividing the lesser of purchases or sales for the fund's fiscal year by the monthly average of the portfolio's net assets. Excluded are securities that mature within a year. A turnover ratio of 100% is the equivalent of a complete portfolio turnover.

12b-1 fee amount that a fund takes from its assets—and thus from its shareholders—to pay for distribution and marketing costs. Usually .25 percent to 1.25 percent of assets. Also called a hidden load.

Unit investment trust fund that buys a portfolio of securities—usually bonds—and normally holds them until maturity.

Volatility fluctuations in the price of a security or index of securities.

Will legal document that provides for how your assets are transferred on your death.

Wilshire 5000 model of all stocks, including those on the New York Stock Exchange, the American Exchange, and over-the-counter. The Wilshire is one of the broadest indexes, and includes over 6,000 stocks.

Yield regular income from a fund, expressed as a percentage of the fund's average net asset value, not including capital gains or losses.

Yield curve graph comparing the interest rates of similar bonds according to their maturities. Usually long-term rates are higher than short-term rates. When short-term rates are higher, there is a negative yield curve.

Yield to maturity yield (as above) plus any certain gains or loss on the price of a bond from now until the time it comes due, expressed as a percentage of the bond's price.

Zero coupon bond bond sold at a fraction of its face value. Its value gradually appreciates as its maturity approaches. No interest is paid to investors, but they must nonetheless pay taxes on the interest accruing annually (except for tax-exempt bonds). Earnings accumulate until maturity.

INDEX

More selected BARRON'S titles:

DICTIONARY OF COMPUTER TERMS, 3rd EDITION
Douglas Downing and Michael Covington
Nearly 1,000 computer terms are clearly explained, and sample programs included. Paperback, $8.95, Canada $11.95/ISBN 4824-5, 288 pages

DICTIONARY OF FINANCE AND INVESTMENT TERMS,
3rd EDITION, *John Downs and Jordan Goodman*
Defines and explains over 3000 Wall Street terms for professionals, business students, and average investors.
Paperback $9.95, Canada $13.95/ISBN 4631-5, 544 pages

DICTIONARY OF INSURANCE TERMS, 2nd EDITION *Harvey W. Rubin*
Approximately 3000 insurance terms are defined as they relate to property, casualty, life, health, and other types of insurance.
Paperback, $9.95, Canada $13.95/ISBN 4632-3, 416 pages

DICTIONARY OF REAL ESTATE TERMS, 3rd EDITON
Jack P. Friedman, Jack C. Harris, and Bruce Lindeman
Defines over 1200 terms, with examples and illustrations. A key reference for anyone in real estate. Comprehensive and current.
Paperback, $10.95, Canada $13.95/ISBN 1434-0, 224 pages

ACCOUNTING HANDBOOK, *Joel G. Siegel and Jae K. Shim*
Provides accounting rules, guidelines, formulas and techniques etc. to help students and business professionals work out accounting problems. Hardcover: $29.95, Canada $38.95/ISBN 6176-4, 832 pages

REAL ESTATE HANDBOOK, 3rd EDITION
Jack P. Freidman and Jack C. Harris
A dictionary/reference for everyone in real estate. Defines over 1500 legal, financial, and architectural terms.
Hardcover, $29.95, Canada $39.95/ISBN 6330-9, 810 pages

HOW TO PREPARE FOR THE REAL ESTATE LICENSING
EXAMINATIONS-SALESPERSON AND BROKER, 4th EDITION
Bruce Lindeman and Jack P. Freidman
Reviews current exam topics and features updated model exams and supplemental exams, all with explained answers.
Paperback, $11.95, Canada $15.95/ISBN 4355-3, 340 pages

BARRON'S FINANCE AND INVESTMENT HANDBOOK,
3rd EDITION, *John Downes and Jordan Goodman*
This hard-working handbook of essential information defines more than 3000 key terms, and explores 30 basic investment opportunities. The investment information is thoroughly up-to-date. Hardcover $29.95, Canada $38.95/ISBN 6188-8, approx. 1152 pages

FINANCIAL TABLES FOR MONEY MANAGEMENT
Stephen S. Solomon, Dr. Clifford Marshall, Martin Pepper, Jack P. Freidman and Jack C. Harris
Pocket-sized handbooks of interest and investment rate tables used easily by average investors and mortgage holders. Paperback
Real Estate Loans, 2nd Ed., $6.95, Canada $8.95/ISBN 1618-1, 336 pages
Mortgage Payments, 2nd Ed., $5.95, Canada $7.95/ISBN 1386-7, 304 pages
Bonds, 2nd, $5.95, Canada $7.50/ISBN 4995-0, 256 pages
Comprehensive Annuities, $5.50, Canada $7.95/ISBN 2726-4, 160 pages
Canadian Mortgage Payments, 2nd Ed., Canada $8.95/ISBN 1617-3, 336 pages
Adjustable Rate Mortgages, 2nd Ed., $6.95, Canada $8.50/ISBN 1529-0, 288 pages

Barron's Educational Series, Inc.
250 Wireless Boulevard, Hauppauge, NY 11788
Call toll-free: 1-800-645-3476
In Canada: Georgetown Book Warehoude
34 Armstrong Ave., Georgetown, Ontario L7G 4r9
Call toll-free: 1-800-247-7160

R 2/94

More selected BARRON'S titles:

DICTIONARY OF ACCOUNTING TERMS
Siegel and Shim
Nearly 2500 terms related to accounting are defined.
Paperback, $10.95, Can. $14.50 (3766-9)

DICTIONARY OF MARKETING TERMS
Imber and Toffler
Nearly 3000 terms used in the marketing and ad industry are defined.
Paperback, $11.95, Can. $15.95 (1783-8)

DICTIONARY OF BANKING TERMS
Fitch
Nearly 3000 terms related to banking, finance and money management.
Paperback, $10.95, Can. $14.50 (3946-7)

DICTIONARY OF BUSINESS TERMS, 2nd EDITION
Friedman, general editor
Over 6000 entries define business terms.
Paperback, $11.95, Can. $15.95 (1530-4)

BARRON'S BUSINESS REVIEW SERIES
These guides explain topics covered in a college level business course.
Each book: paperback
ACCOUNTING, 2nd EDITION. *Eisen.* $11.95,Can.$15.95 (4375 8)
BUSINESS LAW, 2nd EDITION. *Hardwicke and Emerson.* $11.95,
Can. $15.95 (1385 9)
BUSINESS STATISTICS, 2nd EDITION. *Downing and Clark.* $11.95,
Can. $15.95 (1384-0)
ECONOMICS, 2nd EDITION. *Wessels.* $11.95, Can. $15.95 (1392 1)
FINANCE, 2ndEDITION. *Groppelli and Nikbakht.* $11.95,
Can. $15.95 (4373 1)
MANAGEMENT, 2nd EDITION. *Montana and Chanulv.* $11.95,
Can. $15.95 (1549 5)
MARKETING, 2nd EDITION. *Sandhusen.* $11.95, Can. $15.95 (1548-7)
QUANTITATIVE METHODS. *Downing and Clark.* $10.95,
Can. $14.95 (3947 5)

BARRON'S FOREIGN LANGUAGE BUSINESS DICTIONARIES
Six bilingual dictionaries translate about 3000 terms not found in most
foreign phrasebooks:
Each book, paperback: $9.95, Can. $11.95
FRENCH FOR THE BUSINESS TRAVELER, ISBN 1768-4
GERMAN FOR THE BUSINESS TRAVELER, ISBN 1769-2
ITALIAN FOR THE BUSINESS TRAVELER, ISBN 1771-4
KOREAN FOR THE BUSINESS TRAVELER, ISBN 1772-2
RUSSIAN FOR THE BUSINESS TRAVELER, ISBN 1784-6
SPANISH FOR THE BUSINESS TRAVELER, ISBN 1773-0

All prices are in U.S. and Canadian dollars and subject to change without notice.
At your bookseller, or order direct adding 10% postage (minumum charge $3.75,
Canada $4.00) N.Y. residents add sales tax.   ISBN PREFIX 0-8120

Barron's Educational Series, Inc.
250 Wireless Boulevard, Hauppauge, NY 11788
Call toll-free: 1.800.645.3476
In Canada: Georgetown Book Warehouse
34 Armstrong Ave., Georgetown, Ontario L7G 4R9
Call toll-free: 1-800-247-7160

R 2/94

BARRON'S BUSINESS KEYS Each "key" explains approximately 50 concepts and provides a glossary and index. Each book: Paperback, 160 pp., 4 3/16 " x 7", $4.95, Can. $6.50. ISBN Prefix: 0-8120.

Keys for Women Starting or Owning a Business (4609-9)
Keys to Avoiding Probate and Reducing Estate Taxes (4668-4)
Keys to Business and Personal Financial Statements (4622-6)
Keys to Buying a Foreclosed Home (4765-6)
Keys to Buying a Franchise (4484-3)
Keys to Buying and Owning a Home (4251-4)
Keys to Buying and Selling a Business (4430-4)
Keys to Choosing a Financial Specialist (4545-9)
Keys to Conservative Investments (4762-1)
Keys to Estate Planning and Trusts, 2nd Edition (1710-2)
Keys to Financing a College Education, 2nd Edition (1634-3)
Keys to Improving Your Return on Investments (ROI) (4641-2)
Keys to Incorporating (3973-4)
Keys to Investing in Common Stocks (4291-3)
Keys to Investing in Corporate Bonds (4386-3)
Keys to Investing in Government Securities (4485-1)
Keys to Investing in International Stocks (4759-1)
Keys to Investing in Mutual Funds, 2nd Edition (4920-9)
Keys to Investing in Options and Futures (4481-9)
Keys to Investing in Real Estate, 2nd Edition (1435-9)
Keys to Investing in Your 401(K) (1873-7)
Keys to Managing Your Cash Flow (4755-9)
Keys to Mortgage Financing and Refinancing, 2nd Edition (1436-7)
Keys to Personal Financial Planning, 2nd Edition (1919-9)
Keys to Personal Insurance (4922-5)
Keys to Purchasing a Condo or a Co-op (4218-2)
Keys to Reading an Annual Report (3930-0)
Keys to Retirement Planning (4230-1)
Keys to Risks and Rewards of Penny Stocks (4300-6)
Keys to Saving Money on Income Taxes (4467-3)
Keys to Starting a Small Business (4487-8)
Keys to Surviving a Tax Audit (4513-0)
Keys to Understanding Bankruptcy, 2nd Edition (1817-6)
Keys to Understanding the Financial News, 2nd Edition (1694-7)
Keys to Understanding Securities (4229-8)
Keys to Women's Basic Professional Needs (4608-0)

Available at bookstores, or by mail from Barron's. Enclose check or money order for full amount plus sales tax where applicable and 10% for postage & handling (minimum charge $3.75, Can. $4.00) Prices subject to change without notice.

Barron's Educational Series, Inc. • 250 Wireless Blvd.
Hauppauge, NY 11788 • Call toll-free: 1-800-645-3476
In Canada: Georgetown Book Warehouse
34 Armstrong Ave., Georgetown, Ont. L7G 4R9
Call toll-free: 1-800-247-7160   R 5/94